House of the Customer
A blueprint for one-to-one, customer-first, employee-driven business transformation

By Greg Kihlström

What people are saying about
House of the Customer

A blueprint to design best practices, strategies, and techniques to move from deep listening to deep understanding, from powerful statistics to powerful stories. Better metrics and better results are within reach thanks to Greg's craftsmanship.
—**Karen Mangia**
WSJ Best Selling Author & Salesforce Executive

Several insights struck me when reading Greg's latest book: the House of the Customer. First, the importance of focusing on customer experiences beyond the initial marketing and purchasing components, to include multi-channel journey orchestration and importantly, customer service. Second, the idea that data is the connective tissue that drives all of these experiences together in a seamless fashion and the need for building and optimizing a data-based view of customers. Thirdly, Greg captures the unique role that employees have in facilitating these powerful experiences. Greg's book provides a blueprint for thinking holistically about experience in a way that is both insightful and actionable
—**Brian Browning**
Vice President, Technology, Kin + Carta

This book is a must read. From the foundation (Company Culture) to the Roof and all the pillars in between, Greg does a fantastic job laying out the vital components in delivering the best customer experiences.
—**Sara Taheri**
Vice President and Chief Product Owner of Contact Center Transformation and Robotics at Prudential Financial, Inc.

We live in an interconnected world and the recipe for business success is evolving to become more intertwined as well. Business can no longer excel as category leaders with internal silos, paradigms and departments need to evolve to build alignment of vision between Brand, Marketing, CX, HR, and Finance. As Greg artfully guides readers along the journey on customer centricity with his ninth book, he connects the dots between customer experience (CX) and employee experience (EX) and how CX is everyone's job which requires roots in the culture of a business. Everyone from front-line staff to the C-Suite needs to underpin all decisions with the idea of doing what is in the best interests of the customer, not because the business is driving the change but because customers demand that change and we have a duty to shareholders to continue to grow a profitable business into the future. The only way to do this is to meet customers where they are. Applying the concepts contained in the House of the Customer is not just a recommendation but a requirement to breed the trust, loyalty, and greater share of wallet that all founders, owners and executives desire. Greg does a fabulous job of simplifying an array of customer-centric ideas which serve as a blueprint for those just getting started or those looking to continuously improve their businesses position and market-share.
—**Adam Chen**
Chief Marketing Officer, The Amenity Collective

House of the Customer is one of those rare books that not only offers frameworks and philosophies - it is one of those practitioner / operator field manuals that enables practical advice to make progress to grow and scale businesses for those who put customers first. If you want to accelerate and really make a dent in your mission as a customer centered leader, this is a required reading. Plus it's fun, easy, practical and immediately delivers.
—**Carlos Manalo**
Founder, The Office of Experience

Copyright © 2023 by Greg Kihlström.

All rights reserved. In accordance with the US Copyright Act of 1976, the scanning, uploading, and electronic sharing of any part of this book without the permission of the publisher constitute unlawful piracy and theft of the author's intellectual property. If you would like to use material from the book (other than for review purposes), prior written must be obtained by contacting the author. Thank you for your support of the author's rights.

Published by:

The Agile Brand, LLC

3100 Clarendon Boulevard #200

Arlington, VA 22201

https://gregkihlstrom.com

First Edition: January 2023

The publisher is not responsible for websites (or their content) that are not owned by the publisher.

Edited by Duo Storytelling and Janelle Kihlström

Cover design and illustrations by Greg Kihlström

Copyright 2023

ISBN - 9798359571289

Contents

About the Author	8
Acknowledgements	10
Foreword	13
Introduction	19
Part 1: Why We Build	28
Part 2: The House of the Customer	56
Part 3: Building the House	232
Conclusion	279
Appendix	282
References	291

*For my parents,
who built a house and family
with all the love they could possibly give.
I'm forever grateful.*

About the Author

Greg Kihlström is a best-selling author, speaker, and entrepreneur. He currently works with top companies as an advisor on customer and employee experiences as well as digital transformation. He is a two-time CEO and cofounder, having both grown and sold Carousel30 and Digics. A strategist and digital transformation and customer experience advisor, he has worked with some of the world's top brands, including Adidas, Coca-Cola, Dell, FedEx, HP, Marriott, MTV, Starbucks, Toyota, and VMware.

He is a member of the School of Marketing Faculty at the Association of National Advertisers (ANA) and currently serves on the University of Richmond's Customer Experience Advisory Board. Greg was the founding Chair of the American Advertising Federation's National Innovation Committee and served on the Virginia Tech Pamplin College of Business and Trust for the National Mall's Marketing Advisory Boards. He earned his MBA from Quantic School of Business and Technology, is Lean Six Sigma Black Belt certified, is a Certified Agile Coach (ICP-ACC), and holds a certification in Business Agility (ICP-BAF).

Meaningful Measurement of the Customer Experience (2022), Greg's eighth book, provides guidance on how to create a customer-centric culture that prioritizes customer needs while aligning internal teams around a common goal. His seventh book, *The Agile Workforce* (2021), explores the current and future state of the workforce and envisions a future where individuals thrive in a new world of technology-enabled work opportunities, decentralization, and reformed power dynamics between employers and employees. Greg's *The Center of Experience* (2020) talks about how customer and employee experiences can be operationalized within a cohesive brand experience. *The Agile Brand* (2018) follows the evolution of branding from its beginnings to the authentic brand relationship that modern consumers want. It also gives practical examples of how you can create a more modern, agile brand while staying true to your core values. Greg also hosts *The Agile Brand with Greg Kihlström* podcast, in which he discusses brand strategy, marketing, and customer experience with some of the world's leading experts and leaders.

Greg is a regular contributing writer for Forbes (through the Forbes Agency Council) and CMSWire, and he has been featured in publications such as *Advertising Age*, *SmartCEO*, *Website Magazine*, and the *Washington Post*. Greg was named an ICMI 2022 Top 25 CX Thought Leader and was a DC Inno 2018 50 on Fire winner. He's participated as a keynote speaker and panelist at industry events around the world, including MarTech, Internet Week New York, Internet Summit, EventTech, SMX Social Media, CX Forums, Mid-Atlantic Marketing Summit, ABA Bank Marketing Summit, and VMworld. He has guest lectured at several schools, including VCU Brandcenter, Georgetown University, Duke University, American University, University of Maryland, Howard University, and Virginia Tech.

Greg lives in Alexandria, Virginia, with his wife Lindsey.

Acknowledgments

I'm proud to say that this is my eleventh book, and as with my previous ten, there are countless people to thank. I know I'll never get even close to naming them all.

Thanks to Barry Padgett, CEO of leading customer data platform company Amperity, for writing the foreword. I met Barry through an interview for my podcast, and it was clear from the start that we share a common belief in the interconnectedness of the customer and employee experiences.

Thanks to Jesse from Duo Storytelling for the editing work on this book. Also, thank you to Alicia Recco for creating the branding for *The Agile Brand* and inspiring all the design work since, as well as my sister, Janelle Kihlström-Pomery for all of her editing work on this book as well as over the years!

I also want to thank those in the CX community, particularly CXPA, which has been particularly supportive of my work. Thank you to Greg Mehlia, Gabe Smith, Diane Tamagno, Patty Soltis, Lyall Vanatta, Emily Gaylord, Steve Pappas, Mark Michelson, Scott Gilbey, and the many others I've had the pleasure of collaborating with over the last few years.

Thanks also to both Kin + Carta and Office of Experience, two amazing, talented teams I've had the privilege of contributing to while working on this book. Thanks to Carlos Manalo, Brian Browning, Stratton Cherouny, Jason Bowman, Donald Layden, Patrick McCarthy,

Timothy Lyons, Kirk Sagert, Nathan Ley, Ryan Ledoux, Hellen Orwa, and many others.

I would also like to thank all the wonderful podcast guests I've had in the four-plus years of hosting *The Agile Brand with Greg Kihlström*. I've included excerpts from some recent episodes in relevant portions of this book as well. Thanks to the following (and many others): Alex Atzberger, CEO of Optimizely; Anthony Coppedge from IBM; John Nash from Redpoint Global; Sami Nuwar, Wendy Pravda, and Judy Bloch from Medallia; Sara Taheri from Prudential Financial; Paulette Chafe, head of consumer insights and thought leadership at Zendesk; John Estafanous from RallyBright; Jon Ebert from John Deere; Tim Brackney from RGP; and Leon Gilbert and Weston Morris from Unisys. I also want to thank my sponsors, TEKsystems, and in particular, Jason Hayman. Thanks also to Attribution, especially David Hiltner and Cameron Horton. Thank you to the Missing Link team, who helps me with the production of the show: Louise Salas, Hal Schild, Kim Cates, and Basil Ali.

I thank the many others who have helped me through the years to hone the ideas and thoughts shared in this book. These people come from many different eras of my life, but their influence has been and continues to be felt. Thanks to Lisa Nirell, Claudia Silon, Romie Stefanelli, J. G. Staal, Ed Bodensiek, Josh Olson, Adam Chen, Rachael Mahoney, John Burns, Ingrid Vax, Giuseppe Carabelli, Abby See, David Hiltner, Veronique Morrison, Emily Davis, Miranda Opiela, Gail Legaspi-Gaull, Chad Solomonson, Susan Soroko, Steve Blair, Leon Scioscia, Oz Coruhlu, Paul Duning, Cary Hatch, Jean Bright, Tim Lewis, Michael Walsh, Anne Jacoby, Mark Smith, and many, many more.

Thanks to Miro and their amazing software for making it easy to create the charts for this book. Anyone that has worked with me in the last year knows my fondness for the platform.

I also want to thank my wife, Lindsey, for her continuing, and unwavering support in all my ventures, big and small. Every adventure I've been on has been better and richer because she's a part of my life.

Last, but certainly not least, I want to thank my subscribers, readers, listeners, and YOU for picking up this book. It is an honor and a privilege to be able to share my ideas with you, and I hope you take at least some of the ideas and use them to improve your work and your customers' experiences.

Foreword

We all know what a negative customer experience feels like. You buy an item online, then the company sends you an advertisement for the same item. You try to return an item you bought online at the brand's brick-and-mortar store, only to find the cashier has no idea who you are and what should be a seamless interaction suddenly feels like pulling teeth.

On the other hand, we intuitively appreciate a fantastic customer experience, like when you call to check on a refund and the customer service representative immediately recognizes you and the purpose of your call. The rep can then tell you when the refund is going to hit your bank account and solve any sizing or selection issues that may have led you to seek a return.

Getting these interactions right demands a new way of thinking about customer service. Rather than seeking to close tickets as quickly as possible on the way to the next, brands must focus on delivering the best possible experience across the board. The companies that achieve that goal are rewarded with increased customer loyalty and lifetime value, as well as bottom-line and top-line growth — a rarity in any industry.

I've always been obsessed with customer experience, whether as an engineer building end-user software or as an executive running global sales and marketing teams. Now, as the CEO of Amperity, a customer data platform, I'm in the business of delivering the elusive unified view of the customer, using AI and machine learning to help brands connect messy data together and provide the seamless interactions they've long chased.

Great personalized experiences are the North Star for every brand. Greg Kihlstrom has been writing about this subject for years, and when I joined him on The Agile Brand Podcast, we had the chance to discuss our shared obsession. We chatted through the challenges companies face in navigating by that North Star, as well as the benefits such an approach can bring.

For example, a well-known American airline knew delivering the right messaging at key moments could smooth the customer experience. By pulling together data for the first time from bookings, their loyalty program, and mobile app, the airline created a dynamic pre-trip journey that featured personalized messages on itinerary and upsells for the cabin and meal. The new process led to a significant improvement in guest engagement — and ultimately gains in revenue.

In this book, Greg uses the metaphor of a house to describe how successful companies can transform their people, processes, and technology to optimize their customer experience. It's a powerful blueprint — one that demands a strong foundation. That foundation is a customer-centric company culture, where strategy is set based on what the data reveals about customer preferences and behavior, and where customer metrics are everyone's metrics, from marketing to IT and data science, from finance to the leadership team.

As I write this, companies are emerging from a pandemic and staring at a potential recession. Brands have a tough job right now, made more challenging by unprecedented economic and social pressures. Figuring out what the customer wants is hard, and organizing a company to be dynamic and responsive to that demand is even harder.

But the initiative is mission critical, so leaders must take the first step now.

How Employees Impact Customer Experience

Employees are the frontline face of the brand. We often focus on what the customer sees and feels — rightfully so — but forward-thinking brands recognize that getting the customer experience right can create an equal amount of joy for employees. The vast majority of consumer brands employ people who truly do want to serve the customer. Employees want to deliver a great customer experience, and when they don't have the data they need to do so they feel just as frustrated as the customer having the sub-par interaction.

Employees often rely on a series of outdated tools to do their jobs, but even the latest and greatest technology is ineffective without the right data feeding it. When your marketing teams are forced to wait two weeks for the data they need to run a campaign, or when they don't feel like they can trust that the data is accurate, you're losing out on productivity and driving your employees crazy.

The opposite is also true. When those employees — everyone from the data scientists to the finance decision-makers — have an accurate and accessible understanding of the customer, everything changes in how they approach the business. One of my favorite examples is Brooks Running, where customer service reps found that with the right data they were able to solve support tickets before customers could even finish explaining their problems.

To achieve that view of the customer, brands need a solid data foundation. Over the next couple years, the cost of acquiring new customers is going to rise due to inflation, the deprecation of third-party cookies, and the walled gardens at Google and Facebook becoming more expensive to scale. When data is properly organized and accessible, companies can get ahead of their customer needs and drive them toward loyalty programs, increasing retention and customer lifetime value.

Today's brands — from retailers and restaurants to financial services and football teams — have more data than ever to work with, but they're still failing to bridge the data gap standing between them and what their customers want. Amperity recently conducted a survey that found over 80% of respondents collected demographic, sentiment, and identity data, and nearly two-thirds wanted to add an even richer mix. However, brands need to use what they already have — 77% of decision-makers think they underutilize customer data.

Customer data is inherently chaotic, assembled over a long time from various systems across different teams, existing in different formats, and subject to change as the customer goes through life and moves to a different address or gets a new phone number. That leads to several issues. It's difficult to make an interaction with a customer feel cohesive when they're buying in-store, browsing a website, logging a support ticket, or picking an item up curbside. IT teams need to marry all of those siloed data sources — from marketing clouds to e-commerce tools to point of sale systems — to make it easy for employees to access when they need it, not days or weeks later.

Employee experiences and customer experiences are much more connected than is commonly understood. Ultimately, it comes back to first principles. As customers ourselves, what would we love from a brand? How do we expect the brands we love to know and treat us? When we answer those questions, the customer experience improves in tandem with the employee experience.

Building The House of the Customer

The good news for companies is that you don't have to boil the ocean all at once. A great first step would be to bring your team leaders to the table and agree that re-focusing your business on the customer experience is the most important thing you can do long-term. Then pick some short-term use cases that make sense and get some wins on the board.

Stop advertising items to customers who've already purchased the product. You're not only burning money with that bloated programmatic budget, you're also burning the customer experience and making it clear to customers that your brand doesn't truly understand them.

Stop making customers have to recount their history with the brand in a service interaction, which is the equivalent of seeing someone at a party who remembers your name and what you talked about last time you met but you treat them like a stranger.

Instead, help customers feel good about giving you their personal details when they transact by using what you know about them to tailor their experience to their preferences. Make your customers feel *seen*.

By the time you close this book, Greg will have provided you with a blueprint for understanding and serving your customers. I implore you to follow it and ensure your fellow company leaders are equally invested in the effort. Your result will be loyal customers, enthusiastic employees, and the type of sustained revenue growth that only a customer-centric approach can deliver.

Good luck.

Barry Padgett
Chief Executive Officer
Amperity

Introduction

The loftier the building, the deeper must the foundation be laid.
—Thomas A. Kempis

By 1935, one of the greatest architects of all time was considered past his prime. A new, more modern technique was replacing his organic style. By the late 1960s, Frank Lloyd Wright, pioneer of the Prairie School of architecture, had only built a few buildings and appeared to be running out of inspiration. He was busy dealing with personal struggles after his affair with a client and separation from his wife.[1]

Enter a client that would commission a masterpiece. Edgar J. Kaufmann, the owner of the Kaufmann's department store in Pittsburgh, which was later owned by Macy's, wanted a weekend home at a former "summer camp" for his employee retreats. Kaufmann's son, Edgar Kaufmann Jr., had studied under Wright in Wisconsin a year earlier, and after being introduced in person, the Kaufmanns asked him to build their vacation home, Fallingwater.[2]

The Cost of Rushed Design

Legend has it that Wright repeatedly lied to Kaufmann, saying he was hard at work on the designs without having actually started. Finally fed up, Kaufmann surprised the architect by calling him for a visit. In the two-hour span between Kaufmann telling Wright he was on his way and actually arriving to see the designs, Wright drew up the plans.[3]

In that process, Wright made several decisions that were both controversial and contrary to Kaufmann's original request. For instance, while the building site included a brilliant view of a waterfall, Wright chose to put the building at the top of the waterfall rather than below it. This decision led to its iconic relationship with water—it flows through the house rather than being a part of the scenery.

The dramatic, cantilevered design provided wonderful views while immersing occupants in the surrounding nature, but Kaufmann's contractors had concerns about the design feature.

Serious structural flaws caused the first-floor cantilever to sag, which required steel supports to be added in the 1990s, and some more extensive reworking needed to be done in 2002.

The complexity of the design also meant that what was supposed to be a $25,000 project ended up costing the Kaufmanns $155,000, or about $2.5 million in today's dollars, making it one of Wright's most expensive designs.[4] One can't help but wonder if a little more planning could have prevented that cost overrun.

The Reward of Inspiration

The fact remains, however, that Fallingwater is a landmark of design that has stood the test of time and is one of Frank Lloyd Wright's greatest achievements. Flaws in the process aside, you must admire Wright's commitment to his vision, as well as Kaufmann's trust in the design process.

Great work spawns more great work. Although he wasn't as prolific after Fallingwater, Frank Lloyd Wright would go on to design several other renowned works, including the Guggenheim Museum in New York.

Building things can be incredibly rewarding, but the process is rarely easy. It also takes many people working together, sometimes amid competing priorities. Deadlines can be a good thing. Would Fallingwater have had a better design if Frank Lloyd Wright spent more time on it? No one can truly know.

Building Your Own House

Ever feel like your current project could have used more design time, a more realistic engineering approach, or a little more collaboration between the right people?

Of course, we're not talking about architecture, interior design, or anything like that. Instead, we're going to use the metaphor of building a house to discuss how brands provide great experiences for their customers. Why? Because they have a lot in common.

First, we want to *welcome* our customers, advocates, and evangelists into our brand. What better way to do that than by building a house for them? After all, we're asking for a lot from them: their trust, loyalty, and hard-earned dollars.

Second, like a house, a brand should be built to withstand external forces and endure without needing to be fundamentally redesigned. (Of course, it might benefit from the occasional cosmetic refresh.)

Building a House of the Customer means that we're creating something that is memorable, valuable, and built to last. Not every customer will stay for a lifetime, but a house is a good way of visualizing something that provides a *meaningful* experience to everyone involved, including the employees that work to deliver the experience.

All that said, the metaphor only stretches so far. There might be some areas where the house analog works better than others. I hope you stick with me through some of the tougher areas because it's a concept that can translate to successful execution across an organization.

This Is Based on Research . . . and Experience

I'm thankful for the abundance of research on building customer-centric organizations and the move to a first-party data approach. I have included the most recent studies, surveys, and reports available, prioritizing those completed within two years of this book's publication.

Additionally, I have been privileged to work with several organizations of varying sizes (Fortune 50, 100, 500, and 1,000) and assisted with strategy creation, solution finding, and delivering the types of initiatives this book describes. I am committed to being both a writer-researcher and a practitioner; I want my insights to be more than theoretical. My hope is that this makes the concepts on the page more actionable, insightful, and beneficial.

Marketing Continues to Evolve—So Does Customer Experience

Although 2020 was a challenging year for all brands, marketing spend seems to be back on track for growth. A recent Nielsen report estimates advertising spend grew from $57.4 billion in 2020 to $74 billion in 2021 and predicts growth of nearly 10% for 2022.[5] In fact, the internet economy itself has grown seven times faster than the overall US economy over the past four years, accounting for 12% of the US GDP.[6]

The COVID-19 pandemic didn't inhibit new business creation either. Quite the opposite. According to the US Census Bureau, 2021 saw the greatest growth in new businesses created over the last fifteen years, and 68% more than average filings during the five years before the pandemic,[7] with 5.4 million new businesses started that year.[8]

Despite this, pragmatism is growing over how these dollars are spent, with return on investment (ROI) being particularly emphasized. This pragmatism can sometimes be at odds with the growing understanding that both customer experience and employee experience are material to the bottom line. Customer-centric companies are 60% more profitable than companies that aren't,[9] and 87% of leaders agree that prioritizing employee happiness provides a competitive advantage.[10] Additionally, customer experience (CX) has become one of the leading points of differentiation in competitive industries, and category leaders are almost always leagues ahead in CX compared to those ranking third and fourth in their spaces.

Getting to that point takes work, and not just once. It takes a strong, sustained effort that is supported by leaders, driven by employees, felt by customers, and shared with the world. That's what this book is here to do.

We are going to talk about how to build our companies around customers so that everyone—our customers and employees—can benefit while bringing long-term revenue and value to the business itself. It takes big thinking, a lot of planning, great execution, and a team that is motivated and engaged to do amazing things.

Who This Book Is For

Customer centricity falls within many domains of the modern enterprise. Certain teams and departments may have *customer* in their titles, but CX is everyone's job, even if there is a specific person (such as a CX officer or chief customer officer) responsible for setting the strategy.

Although I have written several books geared toward helping CX professionals, this book is meant to marry my roots in the marketing world with the field of CX. CX practitioners will find some helpful ideas in here, as will those in marketing strategy, digital experience, customer data, marketing operations, and other related areas.

This book falls in the sweet spot between marketing and CX. Although this isn't a book that explores the convergence of the two, I see common ground for the two audiences.

My goal is for this book to be a practical resource for any practitioner providing personalized experiences. Although there is some theory in here, and plenty of research to back up my points, I want to give you the tools to create a robust strategy, infrastructure, governance structure, and plan that will improve your ability to provide meaningful and personalized experiences for your customers.

What This Book Is Not

Although this book is aimed at helping marketing leaders and those tasked with creating customer-centric experiences, this is not a handbook on marketing basics. Instead, it is a blueprint of the tools, practices, and mindset needed to perform omnichannel personalized customer experiences well.

Using the ideas and outlines in this book, you can create a strategy that matches your organization's unique characteristics, consumer sets, existing processes, infrastructure, and business goals. All the building blocks are here, as is a framework to start stacking them up.

Every organization is different, so their "houses" will look a little different. Nonetheless, they will still share fundamental design similarities, including what is used to construct them.

What We Will Cover

In part 1, "Why We Build," I outline the rationale behind needing the House of the Customer. This is mostly rooted in articulating your "North Star," or the guiding principles, strategies, and tactics that visionary brands use to provide the personalized experiences customers increasingly demand.

In part 2, I detail the components of the House of the Customer piece by piece. I cover each piece of the house, from roof to foundation. This includes the following:

- Processes and systems
- Business objectives
- The fundamentals of understanding, serving, and listening to the customer
- A customer-centric culture
- Customer relationships

Finally, part 3 explores how to build a House of the Customer, with practical advice on getting started, securing stakeholder buy-in, and measuring success.

I have also included several tools and resources I created based on personal experience and third-party research. These include a maturity model with a comparison reference and a prioritization model that uses the components of the House of the Customer as measurement points. In addition, I briefly revisit the company culture framework I introduced in *The Center of Experience* (2020).

Where This Fits among My Other Books

This book is the final book in a trilogy that explores CX. *The Center of Experience* (2020) describes in detail how to set up a Center of Excellence around both CX and employee experience (EX). Toward the end of this book, I detail the benefits of setting up a Center of Experience and how it relates to a House of the Customer.

Meaningful Measurement of the Customer Experience (2022) focuses, as the name suggests, almost exclusively on the *customer* experience and how to measurement it. It expands on the measurement and analytics components within the Center of Experience.

How the Books Fit Together

Figure 0.1, How the Books Fit Together

These books are like Russian nesting dolls. As pictured in Figure 0.1 above, this book, *The House of the Customer*, is the largest nesting doll, as it focuses on the biggest picture of the three. It's followed by *The Center of Experience*, with *Meaningful Measurement of the Customer Experience* as the smallest, center-most nesting doll.

Additional Resources

You can find some related resources, as mentioned within the chapters that follow, available on my website, https://gregkihlstrom.com/, or directly at https://houseofthecustomer.com/.

Part 1: Why We Build

If you want to build a ship, don't drum up people to collect wood and don't assign them tasks and work, but rather team them to long for the endless immensity of the sea.
—Antoine de Saint-Exupery

The town of Burkburnett seemed an unlikely place for a skyscraper, but as fortune would have it, a booming economy and several optimistic townspeople paved the way for just such a thing. Around 20,000 people flocked to the small town in Wichita County, Texas, in 1912. Word had spread of an oil field that promised high-paying jobs like those in so many boomtowns in similar areas.

The Newby-McMahon Building would be a monument to the town's new wealth, according to J. D. McMahon, who raised $200,000 (just shy of three million in today's dollars) to accommodate the influx of new businesses and professionals.[11] This building would put Burkburnett, Texas, on the map, and both the town's leaders and its growing population were in full support of it.

There was just one catch. Although the drawings of the building *looked* as though they had the dimensions of a skyscraper, there was something amiss. The legal documents McMahon submitted (and ultimately used in his dispute with outraged townspeople) stated the building would be 480 *inches* tall instead of 480 *feet* tall. In fact, McMahon was careful to never verbally state that the building would be

480 feet tall, and no one responsible for approving the documentation seemed to notice.

So, because of one word, Burkburnett, Texas, is home to a four-story skyscraper, known by many as the world's smallest.[12] This elaborate con stands in the town of Burkburnett, Texas, to this day.

There are several lessons to learn from this, but what I want to focus on is the need to start any transformative effort with the right plan. This includes a solid strategy, the right team for that job, and yes, the right *measurements* to ensure success. Starting a digital transformation initiative, especially one that may take years, millions of dollars, and countless hours of staff and contractor time to complete, requires that you set the right course from the start.

But let's back up first. You are likely reading this because you are either about to start a customer-focused transformation or are already halfway through. Why are you embarking on a change initiative in the first place? We'll explore this from several perspectives in the pages that follow, but here's a brief overview.

Consumers Demand More

Although 75% of consumer-facing brands claim to have good or excellent personalized customer experiences, a recent report by Twilio that surveyed 3,450 consumers around the world found that less than half (48%) agree.[13]

On my podcast, I interviewed Paulette Chafe, head of Customer Insights and Thought Leadership at Zendesk, one of the world's leading customer service management platforms. We discussed the "Zendesk Customer Experience Trends Report 2022," which found that 48% of customers in North America had higher customer service expectations after 2021.[14] Here's what Paulette had to say about that:

A lot of other companies are also reporting this increase in consumer and customer expectations. Part of this has to do with the fact consumers are owning more technology, and consumers are spending more time online, online shopping, online using social. So, they're comfortable in digital channels. We saw, in our research alone, that almost 25% of people spend five hours a day online doing various activities for personal reasons, and it's not just the younger generations. It's well across the board. Consumer comfort level and their savviness and . . . their expectations have just grown based on their experiences, and I think that's really what we're seeing right now. It's almost like it's a tipping point.[15]

Sounds like this is a challenge and opportunity that isn't going anywhere any time soon!

Change Is the Only Constant

We hear talk about how things are changing faster in our world, but as early as 500 BC, Heraclitus stated, "the only constant in life is change." Though this might seem to only grow truer each day, we can take comfort in the fact that this is how things have always been.

What matters here is not how quickly we react, but the methods and approaches we take to adapt and improve. Simply being reactive doesn't always generate the best results.

When talking about why we must build a transformative culture and a House of the Customer, we need to approach change as a given. We can't ever "set it and forget it"—at least not if we plan to be successful.

There is a long list of companies that tried that approach and ultimately failed to keep up with change. Kodak had a working digital camera as early as 1975 yet failed to capitalize on the trend when the timing was right.[16] Blockbuster turned down the chance to buy Netflix in 2000.[17] The list goes on.

The companies that thrive have kept pace with change, even reinventing themselves when necessary. IBM, known for decades as a hardware business, turned into a software and consulting services company in the 1990s.[18] Nintendo was founded in 1889 as a playing card company before transforming into one of the most successful video gaming companies.[19]

Competition Approaches from Every Angle

The word *disruption* is thrown around a lot and has been for a while. We've heard about Uber disrupting the taxi industry, Amazon disrupting brick-and-mortar retail, and Netflix disrupting the $10 billion video rental industry.[20]

But disruption takes many forms, both small and large. Competition can come from both longstanding rivals and upstarts that focus on a niche within a larger industry.

One of the recurring themes in this book is the need to balance business value, customer needs, and long-term agility. All of this helps businesses stay competitive, no matter what occurs.

Employees Need Purpose

We have seen the cost of employees who feel as though their jobs lack purpose. What many have called the Great Resignation has caused a shift in employment, with many leaving their jobs and rethinking what they want in their careers.

One of the major points I want readers to take away is that it's a win-win situation when we steer our organizations toward customer centricity. I believe that being customer focused can not only benefit customers but provide a greater purpose for employees.

So whose job is it to play a pivotal role in the transformation and continued optimization of the customer experience? According to the 2022 edition of the "Salesforce Marketing Intelligence Report," which surveyed over 2,500 marketers worldwide, 80% of marketers say their organization is the leader in CX initiatives.[21] This is in addition to the many CX teams being added as key stakeholders as global CX technology spend is expected to reach $641 in 2022.[22]

In fact, the size of the CX industry is estimated to grow at least 15% annually from 2021 to 2028.[23]

It is not just marketers or CX teams that play a key role in delivering great personalized experiences. Everyone in an organization has a part to play in building and sustaining the House of the Customer. The most successful organizations understand this and make customer centricity just as much a part of their employee experience as it is part of the customer experience.

Conclusion

So why do we build better customer experiences? We build because consumers demand it, the market demands it, and the future of our brands depends on it. In the next section, we will explore what to look for as you build your House of the Customer. We'll frame this in terms of a North Star that will guide us.

1.1 Our North Star

The function of an ideal is not to be realized but, like that of the North Star, to serve as a guiding point. —Edward Abbey

Polaris A, a supergiant star about 323 light-years from Earth and about six times the mass of our sun, is one of three stars that form a single point of light commonly referred to as Polaris—the North Star.[24] It is called that because it is almost perfectly aligned with our North Pole, meaning its position in the sky barely shifts.

This fixed position of the North Star has helped countless people navigate in the Northern Hemisphere for the last several hundred years.

Just as the North Star is a point of reference for all those who wish to navigate by it, we will use the concept of the North Star to define the fixed goal we're striving to achieve. Although our methods of achieving that North Star goal may change, it won't change the goal itself, so we need to choose it wisely. There may be many other smaller and more immediate goals that help get us where we need to go, but they are not one of our North Star goals.

The Concepts Shaping Our North Star

Before discussing the four components of our North Star, I'd like to cover the elements that shape it. We will continue to add more details to each of these concepts, but I'll briefly introduce them for the time being.

The Competitive Force of Experience

CX continues to be a growing force in how brands make decisions, and numbers show that it's strategically important. Back in 2017, Gartner found that more than two-thirds of marketers responsible for CX said their companies competed based on CX.[25] Research by Emplifi in early 2022 found that 77.3% of brands believe CX is a key competitive differentiator.[26]

The competitive force of customer experience as a point of differentiation seems to only be growing in influence.

The Personalization Imperative

Customers demand personalized experiences. Salesforce's survey of 6,000 consumers found that two-thirds of them expect companies to understand their needs and expectations.[27] For brands with hundreds or even millions of customers, this isn't possible on a one-to-one level. Thus, personalization through automation, artificial intelligence, and next-best-action approaches are essential to keeping up.

The Pressure of Data Privacy and Regulation

Consumer data privacy is at the top of everyone's minds and shapes our approach to building a House of the Customer. The General Data Protection Regulation, or GDPR, was first put into effect on May 25, 2018, and is the toughest, most restrictive consumer data privacy regulation to date.[28] Other jurisdictions have followed suit, including the state of California with its California Consumer Privacy Act (CCPA), which came into effect in January 2020.[29]

There has also been some industry self-regulation, with more to come. Apple and Microsoft have taken steps toward fighting the use of third-party cookies, and Google is preparing to follow. More on this in subsequent chapters.

The Sustainable Business Model

Sustainability takes many forms in business. Putting aside environmental responsibilities, a business has a responsibility to all its stakeholders to create a brand with a loyal customer base, stable employee retention, and yes, even an eye toward corporate social responsibility.

To this end, research from Deloitte and Touche found that customer-centric companies were 60% more profitable than companies that were less focused on the customer.[30] Another study found that 64% of companies with a customer-focused CEO were more profitable than their competitors.[31] When you add that profitability to the other long-term effects that a focus on customers brings, it is a win for both shareholders and other stakeholders, creating greater sustainability.

With that said, let's talk about the components of the North Star that will guide us in building our House of the Customer.

One-to-One Versus Segment Personalization

It is important to note the difference between a true one-to-one personalized experience and personalizing content and experience based on customer segments. Although the latter is beneficial, true one-to-one is exactly what it sounds like: every individual is considered uniquely, and the content, offers, and actions shown are individualized to that user instead of applied to anyone who fits a predefined segment.

Later in the book, we're going to discuss the difference between customer journey orchestration and a one-to-one next-best-action approach. Although orchestration based on audience segments can improve customer satisfaction and customer loyalty, the numbers behind true one-to-one are compelling.

A Forrester study on Pega's one-to-one next-best-action approach showed that a set of companies in the $25 billion revenue range using this approach increased their revenue by $677 million on average, avoided $578 million in churn, and attributed nearly 0.9% of direct revenue to next-best-action.[32]

Although your organization might not be ready for one-to-one just yet, it is important to understand how to get there.

Our North Star

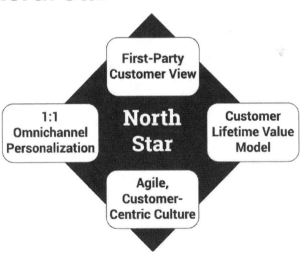

Figure 1.1.1, Our North Star

Let's start by talking about our North Star (Figure 1.1.1), or the ultimate goal of great personalized experiences. This can be broken down into four main goals and outcomes:

1. ***One-to-one omnichannel personalization.*** Every customer has a unique experience tailored to their needs. That experience is tailored from the time they become aware of a product or service until long after they purchase
2. ***First-party customer view.*** Brands have a thorough understanding of their customers and governance over customers' data privacy needs.
3. ***Customer lifetime value model.*** Brands have a thorough understanding of what channels, tactics, offers, and messaging motivate customers and contribute greater value over the customer lifetime.
4. ***Agile, customer-centric culture.*** Driven by a culture of agility, the organization continuously improves its outcomes through systematic improvements in process and delivery.

Being Realistic about Results

Finally, before we explore each of these points in more detail, I want to emphasize one more aspect of the North Star. Just as Polaris guided navigators to their destinations, the North Star for your transformation efforts should serve as a guide. That doesn't mean you need to get there right away.

Every organization has its own strengths and weaknesses, so the important thing is to keep your North Star in sight and always be moving closer to it.

To reinforce this, I've introduced a maturity model you can use to determine your current growth position. This will help you be realistic about your organization's growth and results over time. We'll get to that in the third part of this book.

In the chapters that follow, we will explore each of these in more depth, starting with one-to-one omnichannel personalization.

1.2 One-to-One Omnichannel Personalization

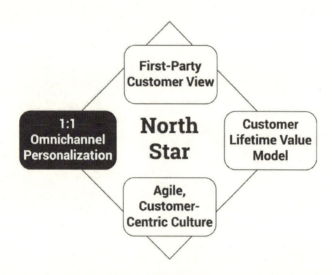

Figure 1.2.1, One-to-One Omnichannel Personalization

Let's look at the first aspect of our North Star: one-to-one omnichannel personalization (Figure 1.2.1). When we use this term, we mean that in an ideal situation, every individual customer has experiences that are tailored for them. Their individual preferences, browsing and order history, location, and other demographic considerations are considered alongside every communication. This is why we call it one-to-one. The brand has a unique, specific relationship with that one individual customer, and that relationship echoes across *every* channel that the individual customer uses to interact with the brand. Therefore, we use the term *omnichannel*. This could be online-only for e-commerce brands, but for many others, it would extend to in-store retail, customer service and support, and anywhere else they interact with the brand and its products or services.

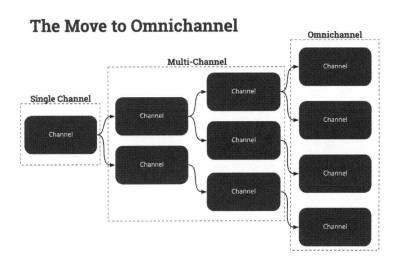

Figure 1.2.2, The Move to Omnichannel

Many more companies are doing what is referred to as "multichannel" personalization (Figure 1.2.2), which is the stage between personalizing a single channel (such as email) and spreading that across platforms and processes toward the goal of all-channels, or *omnichannel*, personalization.

As we'll continue to explore in this book, it is difficult to do omnichannel personalization well. Many organizations are simply not prepared to do this, which is why so many digital transformations are currently in progress. And even for organizations embracing omnichannel personalization, many will not be set up to add more channels into the mix once integration is completed. We will get to some solutions for that in time.

Why It's So Important

There are many reasons why one-to-one personalization is sought after. For instance, 98% of business-to-consumer (B2C) companies recently surveyed by Twilio say that personalization increases customer loyalty, and 83% of consumers surveyed agree with that assessment.[33] In other words, brands *need* one-to-one personalization to grow their business, and consumers *want* it because it provides more seamless access to the products and services they want and need.

Additionally, customer behavior shows that becoming more omnichannel, or at least multichannel, in our approaches is important. Customers are changing channels at an increasing rate. In the chart below, you can see that the number of channels used by customers to search and buy has increased 300% from two to six between 2007 and 2022.[34] Moreover, the number of available channels has also increased. This increases the opportunity to reach customers, but it also increases the risk of a disjointed customer experience.

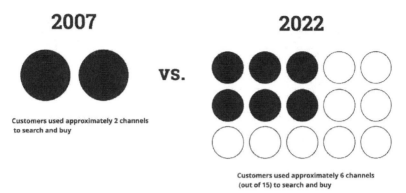

Figure 1.2.3, Channel Switching

Marketers are taking notice of this trend. In Forrester's 2022 report, "The Data Deprecation Challenge and the Promise of Zero-Party Data," two hundred digital marketing decision-makers confirmed that personalized omnichannel or multichannel digital experiences are a key component of their marketing programs.[35]

A key benefit of this personalization: customers spend more money. In fact, Coresight Research found that 71% of consumers surveyed for a 2022 report said that they would shop more often with brands that offered personalized experiences.[36] McKinsey found similar results, showing that companies providing personalization across physical and digital channels can increase revenue by 5% to 15% across their entire customer base.[37]

In the next chapter, we're going to explore the next North Star component, one that enables one-to-one omnichannel personalization: a first-party customer view.

1.3 First-Party Customer View

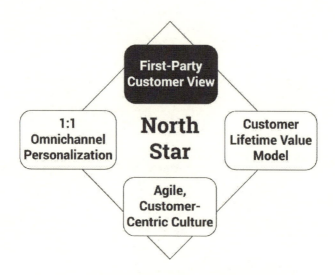

Figure 1.3.1, First-Party Customer View

We'll explore first-party data (and the other types of data and data collection) in much greater detail, but I'll keep it brief. When we refer to *first-party data*, we mean data that is owned and managed by the brand, not an external third-party source.

Between data privacy regulation, industry self-regulation, and the continually growing concerns of consumers themselves, having a first-party customer view is becoming increasingly important. There are also tangible benefits that an organization can derive from delivering better personalized customer experiences.

According to a Forrester Consulting report from early 2022, 99% of respondents say their firms are responding to third-party data deprecation with a first-party data strategy; though, they are finding some aspects more challenging than others.[38]

Data Privacy and Regulation

Internet advertising increased by a whopping 35.4% between 2020 and 2021, in contrast with an increase of only 12.2% in the previous period (2019–2020).[39] Although there are several implications here, it's clear that brands continue to increasingly rely on digital advertising as a means of reaching new audiences. Currently, this advertising is heavily reliant on third-party data sources that create a unified view of a customer across their browsing history, search history, and other records.

Regulations such as the EU's GDPR and the state of California's CCPA, plus industry self-regulation put the current way of doing business at risk.

Although these changes are intended to improve how an individual's data is used, there are implications for business practices that have yet to be solved for.

Apple recently made changes to its iOS operating system to increase user data privacy. According to Meta CFO Dave Whener, these changes are estimated to decrease ad revenues by roughly $10 billion in 2022.[40]

Despite this shift away from third-party cookies and device ID measurements, fewer marketing leaders are planning to adapt their measurement strategies in 2022 (34%) than 2021 (45%).[41] The Interactive Advertising Bureau's interpretation of this is that "the industry is not moving fast enough" to outpace the potential negative effects these changes will have on advertisers.[42]

First-Party Data Collection

If brands can no longer rely on third-party data as a source of information on their customers, they need a much stronger first-party data strategy. This means less (if any) reliance on third-party sources and a need to build a more robust customer data infrastructure. This may be easier for some types of companies than others. For instance, brands that have had direct customer relationships for years have already built their own first-party customer data sets and profiles. Other companies that have traditionally had their sales brokered through third parties are now needing to create their own customer data sets.

In their "H1 2022 Market Report," Mediaocean reports that advertisers consider "measurement improvements centered on non-cookie methods" to be the year's most impactful marketing technology innovation.[43] Although the exact timeline of third-party cookie depreciation is unknown—Google is the current holdout here—most brands are not moving quickly enough.

A similar challenge is also occurring with the loss of mobile device ID tracking. Emodo's recent survey of C-level marketers shows that most of them are experiencing decreased marketing effectiveness (80% of respondents) and sales (82% of respondents) because of mobile ID loss.[44]

Stay tuned for much more on this subject. We'll be exploring this in more depth in the "Understanding the Customer" chapter in the next section of the book. Until then, we're going to move to our next North

Star component, which deals with generating value and results for both the customer and the brand.

1.4 Customer Lifetime Value Model

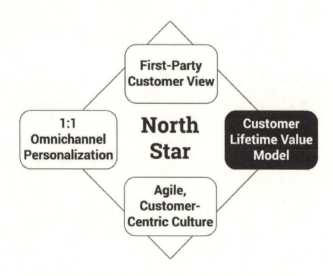

Figure 1.4.1 Customer Lifetime Value Model

We've discussed two of four components of our North Star so far, which have dealt with understanding our customers and delivering the personalized experiences they desire. Our third component answers the all-important question, *How do we measure our success*?

To do this, we want to look at the benefit to both the business as well as the customer, which will give us a view into our long-term, sustainable success. This means our North Star for measurement is customer lifetime value, or CLV.

Many short-term and indicator metrics will be used to gauge success along the way, but the key performance indicator (KPI) to strive for is CLV. Having worked with organizations both large and small, I can tell you that this is a struggle, and the research backs it up. Only 57% of the marketers surveyed in the 2022 Nielsen report are "very confident" or "extremely confident" in their customer lifetime value measurement.[45]

Many brands may need to slowly build toward total CLV as their data collection and measurement sophistication grows.

Multi-Touch Attribution

To get to a better CLV model, we also need to better understand the value of our marketing and advertising efforts. This means that multi-touch attribution, or our ability to understand each communication channel's contribution to a sale, becomes even more important.

So far, the statistics are disappointing at best. Nielsen's "Era of Alignment" report published in 2022 states that global marketers' confidence in full-funnel ROI measurement is only 54%.[46] Clearly there is room for improvement, and we'll discuss both multi-touch attribution and best practices for CLV tracking in more detail later when we discuss listening to our customers. For now, let's move to the final element of our North Star, which focuses on the type of organizational culture needed to support our House of the Customer.

1.5 Agile, Customer-Centric Culture

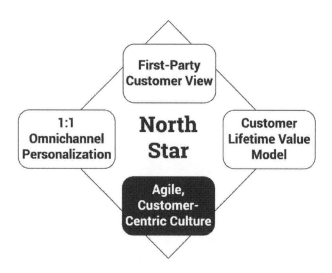

Figure 1.5.1 Agile, Customer-Centric Culture

We've discussed how we understand our customers (first-party customer view), how we deliver them the experiences they desire and demand (one-to-one omnichannel personalization), and how we measure our success (customer lifetime value).

In the fourth and final component of our North Star, we will talk about how the three prior components are delivered operationally. This brings us to the need for an agile, customer-centric culture. Let's start with the first part—agile.

Agility Is No Longer Optional

I used to say that utilizing agile practices is optional, but I've begun to change my mind. I can say now that agile is no longer optional. It has been easy to claim there are alternatives to agile, but time and time again, those alternatives have fallen short.

Once only used by software engineering teams, IT departments, and other technology-centered groups, agile has made inroads in almost every area of business today. Despite this, many companies and teams are still reluctant to adopt agile practices or take steps to formalize the agile practices they already have.

Those that resist agile practices experience gaps in their ability to deliver transformative change initiatives or the improvements needed to keep businesses growing and competitive. In this section, I'm going to discuss why agility is no longer an option and how agile marketing organizations and businesses can better weather whatever storms are on the horizon.

An Eighteen-Month Plan Is an Exercise in Futility

Far be it from me to discourage any company or individual from setting long-term goals. However, there is a difference between setting goals and creating an implementation plan to achieve them.

We simply can't know what will happen eighteen days from now, let alone eighteen months. Creating an agile plan still lets us have a North Star we want to reach, but it adds the realism of possible change. This could be a change in the economy or sociopolitical landscape, a change in the competitive field or industry, or even a change in the workforce or consumer sphere.

When done well, agile planning can be the best of both worlds: it keeps teams focused on creating maximum business value while recognizing that the world changes too quickly to plan exactly how things should be done in the distant future.

How Agility Enhances Your Team's Results

In addition to benefiting your ability to plan and execute important initiatives, agility can help you gain better results from you and your team.

There are several ways to do this. First, agile prioritizes continual reassessment of priority and backlog, allowing you to quickly shift from focuses that aren't working. Additionally, a sprint-based approach where work is performed in small time frames (often two or four weeks) with a formal review process at the end of each (in Scrum, this is referred to as a *retrospective*) allows you to benefit from information you weren't privy to when the campaign or initiative started. Finally, an agile approach allows you to improve your team's process as you go, which can help with both team morale and results.

I spoke with Anthony Coppedge, Principal Agile Digital Sales and Global Transformation lead at IBM about this, and here's what he had to say:

> *We build success one bite at a time, and there's just no secret sauce to that. You go have small successes, and you do it again and again and again, and it grows, but don't let that sound like bottom up. That's not just team agility. That's part of it. But there's also the shift in the way you go about setting your objectives: shifting to client centricity, shifting away from extracting value to creating value. There's a leadership and*

management component, but there's also the team component. It takes both.[47]

All of this adds up to achieving better results from your team's efforts and maintaining a clear focus on creating the most value for the business and the best improvements for the initiative.

How Agility Marketing, IT, and CX Operations

Agile practices also enable more effective execution of your initiatives. This can translate into tangible improvements for your marketing and CX operations.

For instance, adherence to agile practices means that the tasks and items that contribute most to business value will be prioritized over low-impact work. Additionally, agile practices focus on creating a working version of a product, campaign, or initiative as soon as possible. This means there is less time spent waiting to see if all the work your team put into a new initiative will translate into something feasible. Finally, agile practices embrace a mindset of continuous improvement on both results and the methods that generate those results. This means your team will only grow more efficient over time and that the focus is on not only better results but a commitment to improving operational effectiveness over time.

As you can see, agility in all areas of business has a positive impact on strategy, delivery, and the results achieved. If you or your colleagues believe agile practices are optional, it's time to rethink your assumptions.

Customer-Centric Culture

Going hand in hand with an agile approach is a company culture that embraces customer centricity. I like how Built In defines it:

> Company culture can more simply be described as the shared ethos of an organization. It's the way people feel about the work they do, the values they believe in, where they see the company going and what they're doing to get it there. Collectively, these traits represent the personality—or culture—of an organization. A company's culture influences results from top to bottom.[48]

Although not directly stated here, this implies that culture also describes how priorities are set, decisions made, and goals are defined. In other words, what we determine is important defines the culture of our company.

What exactly do we mean by the term *customer centricity*? I'll let Gartner answer that:

> Customer centricity is the ability of people in an organization to understand customers' situations, perceptions, and expectations. Customer centricity demands that the customer is the focal point of all decisions related to delivering products, services, and experiences to create customer satisfaction, loyalty, and advocacy.[49]

What Gartner also implies is that it is not just leaders or even front-line employees who understand the customer in customer-centric culture. *Everyone* in the organization does, and everyone has line of sight on how their role serves the customer. This is incredibly important, even critical, to customer-centric organizations.

As important as agility and customer centricity are on their own, tying them to one another is key. This is why I've done so in our exploration of our North Star. Simply put, it's not enough to understand your customers at one point in time or to understand how to best serve them with personalized experiences. Instead, you need to continually adapt to customers' needs and use best practices to create greater CLV. It is as vital to the customer relationship as it is to the health and future of your brand.

We will explore both agility and customer centricity in much more detail in the last section of the book as we discuss implementing our House of the Customer. Now we are going to move on to detail the individual elements of the House.

Part 2: The House of the Customer

No house should ever be on a hill or on anything.
It should be of the hill. Belonging to it.
Hill and house should live together each the happier for the other.
—Frank Lloyd Wright

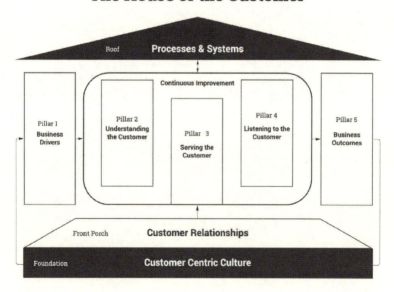

Figure 2.1, The House of the Customer

Now that we've explored our North Star as well as some of the challenges that get in the way of achieving those goals, it's time to start looking at solutions. I like to introduce the metaphor of the House of the Customer (Figure 2.1) as a way of thinking about building your marketing and CX strategy, infrastructure, and more importantly, the way you bring your customer and business needs together into a holistic, continuously improving ecosystem.

With that said, let's start exploring the House of the Customer.

The Foundation: Customer-Centric Culture

We start with the foundation that all this is built on. Although there is a long legacy of top-down, hierarchical management in corporations, the future is more egalitarian. Strong leadership is always needed, but the secret to enabling winning customer experiences that translate into long-term loyalty is enabling employees to help to drive the needed change.

This employee-driven, customer-centric culture will be the topic of the last section on the House of the Customer. It builds on some of the thoughts and concepts from my previous book, *The Center of Experience* (2020), with a focus on a simple concept: delivering a great customer experience is both a motivating factor and reward for employees.

The Five Pillars

Built on our foundation, we have five pillars that support all our customers' activities as well as the strategic needs and outcomes of the organization.

Pillar 1: Business Drivers

The first pillar homes in on business strategy, KPIs, and other needs of the brand that should be factored into decisions about customer experience.

Pillar 2: Understanding the Customer

Next, we have the second pillar, which focuses on the customer. This means collecting data about customers, analyzing and categorizing it, then converting individual users into audience segments to enable mass personalization, orchestration, and much more. This is also where we utilize tools such as customer data platforms (CDPs) to unify the information across platforms and build a holistic view to provide a better brand experience.

Pillar 3: Serving the Customer

This pillar covers all the platforms used to communicate with customers. This includes automation, orchestration, and next-best-action approaches as well as all the considerations and supporting processes and systems that enable personalization.

Pillar 4: Listening to the Customer

Next, we have a portion of our house dedicated to taking all the feedback we gather from Pillar 3 as we endeavor to understand the customer in Pillar 2. Pillar 4, in sum, is all about taking information and using it to better serve customers and improve delivered experiences. We then feed all that information into the next pillar (Pillar 5) to ultimately improve the business.

Pillar 5: Business Outcomes

The final pillar brings us back to the business. You'll notice that the first and fifth pillars form the "walls" containing all the customer-focused areas of the business. Business outcomes include the critical component of measuring, analyzing, and understanding how the quality of customer experience affects the business.

A common theme throughout this book is an agile, iterative process of continuous improvement. Therefore, our fifth pillar is focused on both measurement as well as action. Acting on the data is critical for obvious reasons: it keeps customers happy, it improves long-term profitability, and it keeps us one step ahead of disruptive forces.

Our Front Porch: Customer Relationships

So far, the elements of our House of the Customer have involved internal systems, processes, and platforms that determine strategies as well as delivery and outcomes.

Our front porch is the space we use to maintain and deepen our relationships with customers. In the section on this, we'll talk about methods to acquire the data needed to deliver personalized experiences, as well as the value that those experiences can provide to our customers.

The Roof: Processes and Systems

Last, but certainly not least, we have the roof of our house. This roof includes the processes and systems that enable our House of the Customer to function and serve both external populations (customers and partners) as well as internal ones (employees and stakeholders).

Why is this the roof of our house? Because, when done well, our systems, processes, and governance in general provide protection from disorganization and help us weather unforeseen challenges. It should be noted, that these processes need to include agile approaches based on continuous improvement. This house is continuously being improved over time!

With that brief overview done, let's start exploring our House of the Customer!

2.0 The Foundation: Customer-Centric Culture

*You can dream, create, design, and build the most wonderful place in the world.
But it requires people to make the dream a reality.*
—Walt Disney

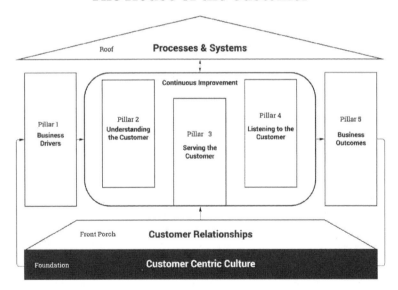

Figure 2.0.1, The Foundation: Customer-Centric Culture

Company culture is important for so many reasons. As we've seen with the Great Resignation, employees who don't see opportunities where they currently work or feel undervalued or unfulfilled are prone to checking out or leaving. To provide more context, the American Psychological Association's "Work and Well-Being" survey found that only 58% of employees feel valued at their current workplace.[50] That means there is a lot of ground to be gained here.

As I write this in mid-to-late 2022, there is talk about the Great Resignation giving way to another phase of the workforce. Economic concerns are causing some belt-tightening which means some of the 11,855,000 job openings in the United States may disappear as we enter a new economic phase.[51]

Regardless of economic conditions, however, company culture is important. In good times, companies with healthy, aligned cultures attract and retain the best possible talent. In bad times, those same companies retain the best of their talent and keep their customers happy.

I call this section of our House of the Customer the foundation because I truly believe that nothing else can be done without the stability of company culture. It is also foundational to customers, employees, and the business itself. Because of this, you need a culture that provides benefits to these three parties.

There is a win-win-win solution here where customers have better experiences, employees gain a greater purpose, and businesses benefit from greater employee retention.

North Star State

According to Hotjar's "State of Customer Experience 2019," of companies that considered themselves "mature" on the CX maturity scale, 41% of them considered themselves "customer-centric," while only 17% of the "least mature" respondents agreed.[52]

This brings us to a key concept of the foundation of our House of the Customer: a customer-centric culture. Let's explore it in more detail.

Motivation and Reward

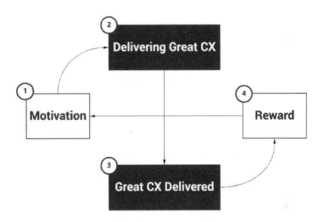

Figure 2.0.2, Motivation and Reward in the Customer-Centric Culture

The idea illustrated in Figure 2.0.1 is that when delivering a great customer experience becomes a motivating factor, it becomes its own reward. This goes along with the premise that employees don't derive all their motivation from extrinsic rewards like salary, bonuses, or other perks. Instead, a good part of their motivation comes from intrinsic motivations—that is, feelings of purpose and fulfillment within their job.

The North Star goal for developing a customer-centric culture is based on the idea that employees will provide additional effort to innovate, solve customer problems, and collaborate with one another when they have a strong sense of purpose. I believe that one primary purpose can be providing the best possible experience to customers. This creates a virtuous cycle like the one pictured above (Figure 2.0.1)

If you are interested in learning more about intrinsic motivation and its relationship to employee engagement and productivity, I recommend *Drive* by Daniel Pink. I also talk about this subject at length in my book *The Center of Experience* (2020).

What We Will Cover

In this section, we are going to explore what we mean by creating a customer-centric culture. I will do this by defining what *customer-first, employee-driven* means and how employees and leadership both play a strong role in fostering that kind of environment.

I will also discuss an additional component of culture: building a culture of innovation. This consistent and intentional approach to innovating and improving is the sign of an intrinsically motivated team.

Let's take a look!

2.0.1 Customer-First, Employee Driven

> *You don't earn loyalty in a day. You earn loyalty day-by-day.*
> —*Jeffrey Gitomer*

Business leaders today struggle with many competing priorities. The needs of customers who demand more personalized experiences must be balanced with the needs of employees who demand a better work experience.

Although this dynamic presents clear challenges, there is also an opportunity to create a win-win for both customers and employees. This situation creates a third win for leaders and the business itself because happier, more engaged employees help create happier and more loyal customers.

This idea has proven itself, so to speak, as more investments are clearly being made to holistically improve customer experience and service within businesses. When I interviewed Paulette Chafe, head of Consumer Insights and Thought Leadership at Zendesk, for my podcast, I asked why she thinks business leaders are leaning so heavily on customer service to drive business growth. Here's what she said:

> *You know, it's interesting times. We discussed how much it's been growing in importance. I tend to classify what I see in the research this year as customer service is the macro business trend. It's earned its time. It's earned its right to be out front*

and center. And I feel like it's happening for a couple of reasons. I would say the number one reason is that customer service has proven itself. There is a proven link between customer service performance and growth. And the business leaders have seen it, and the fact that that justifies and bolsters their request for additional funding, it's a proven thing that business leaders know that they can bet on that's actually going to continue to deliver for them.[53]

Let's explore how this can work and how you can apply this in your leadership approach.

What Do We Mean by *Customer-First?*

Let's start by defining what a *customer-first approach* is and how to create one. As you might guess, it is an approach that asserts that what is right for the customer will translate into the long-term best outcome for the company. This means that the needs of the customer are taken into primary consideration when planning.

At first glance, you would be hard-pressed to find a brand or executive who disagrees with this. However, when it comes to making the necessary decisions, investments, and prioritizations, some organizations clearly practice what they preach, while others stay beholden to short-term, reactionary decisions.

Brands that are truly customer-first put their resources into building customer relationships. This is sometimes at the expense of short-term gains, but always with the understanding that investing in improving the customer experience is key. Coincidentally, most category leaders are defined by a distinct customer experience and loyal consumer relationships.

Customer-first means that when decisions are made, resources are allocated, or strategies are weighed, the relationship with and considerations of their customers are a primary determiner. Although the customers are certainly not the only consideration, they also are not an afterthought when considering profits, shareholder value, or other important factors.

What Is *Employee-Driven?*

Now let's explore what we mean by *employee-driven* and how to achieve it. Although customers are given first consideration, employees must be empowered to drive change and make meaningful contributions in a customer-first approach. This means that team members aren't just told by leaders and managers that customers are important. Instead, those leaders and managers rely on employees for ideas, insights, and action that drives a customer-first approach.

What defines an employee-driven organization? First, there is transparency, meaning employees know key goals and objectives instead of being treated as order-takers. Second, employees take part in solving challenges and achieving goals and objectives. Finally, because of the transparency and autonomy employees are given, they are both motivated to work and innovate their approaches. This drives both better customer results and results for the business itself.

Employees given the autonomy to solve customer problems or suggest better ways of achieving results are going to be happier, more productive, and feel more purpose in their work. This is critical when so many companies are suffering low motivation and high turnover.

How They Work Together

The real magic starts to happen when you can achieve both customer-first and employee-driven approaches and tie them together. I've said before: when customer experience is done well, it is the motivation for great work, and the reward is customer satisfaction and loyalty. The customer and employee aren't the only ones who benefit from this; so do other stakeholders.

Happier employees create happier customers who buy more, buy more often, and refer others. At the same time, motivated employees are more likely to take innovative approaches and to anticipate customers' needs. On top of that, discretionary effort, or an "above and beyond" mentality, that a satisfied employee gives translates to customers who become loyal to a brand and can ultimately become brand ambassadors themselves.

Taking this customer-first, employee-driven approach ensures that these two important factors—your customers and your employees—are integrated into the very foundation of your House of the Customer.

Start with the Right Mindset

Of course, this type of customer-first, employee-driven approach doesn't happen overnight. Organizations that have this mindset have been working at it for a while and make it a part of everything they do. This includes their decisions, the way they train their employees, and the way they prioritize.

I interviewed John Nash, Chief Marketing and Strategy Officer from industry-leading customer data platform provider Redpoint Global, about the mindset of customer-centric organizations. Here's what he said:

> *The mindset of being consumer-centric is the number one priority, and in healthcare, I think Mayo Clinic is a great exemplar of making that consumer centricity a reality, and*

they've done it with their mindset for over one hundred years. It's possible to be entrepreneurial, competitive, idealistic, and serve patients individually all at the same time. And that's a great mindset for today's times if you think about the entrepreneurial dimension. It's being agile, being fast, and identifying those high-value use cases where you can use a data-driven approach to drive results and be competitive.

There's fierce competition for the biggest share of consumer in healthcare. Healthcare organizations are competing with retailers like Amazon and a lot of nontraditional healthcare players. And consumers are picking winners based on a level of personalization. You know Triple Aim—or this three-part set of driving outcomes up, cost down, and providing better patient satisfaction—doesn't have to be a set of conflicting objectives. The technology exists today to achieve that at scale, both digitally and physically. It's arrived, so embrace it. If you're consumer-centric and you focus on that kind of mindset around it, you will be successful.[54]

Why is this enterprise-wide customer-centric culture so important, you ask? Because experience matters every single time—so much so that Lacek Group and Sitecore's recent survey of global consumers showed that 44% of respondents had stopped engaging with a loyalty program because of a single bad experience.[55] That means that no matter how good a channel may perform or how well your team is trained, a single bad experience with one individual could mean the difference between losing or keeping a loyal customer.

The Role of Leadership

A customer-first, employee-driven mindset starts with leaders who set the tone and walk the talk. Leadership should demonstrate a customer- and employee-focused mindset in decision-making and prioritizing initiatives, as well as in the empathy they show in their work and the words they use. There seems to be consensus on this, with 70% of company leaders saying that improvements in employee experience can lead to gains in customer experience that drive revenue gains.[56]

It then falls on leaders to gain buy-in and adoption of customer-centric culture with their employees. When I interviewed Sami Nuwar, Director of Customer Experience Advisory at industry-leading CX and EX platform Medallia, about how leaders both lead by example and gain employee buy-in, here's what he said:

> *The people in the organization take their behavioral cues from their leadership, and when we hear our CEO talk about customer experience in a meaningful way, it resonates through all layers of management. When we see or hear them exhibiting certain behaviors, we tend to emulate them. The organization and organizational behavior are a reflection of the leadership.*
>
> *I'll give you a perfect example of that. The CEO of a company I can't mention by name hosted a leadership meeting covering the usual business topics. You know, essentially our inaugural business review. "We're going to cover the usual topics of performance around profitability" and so on and so forth. So, he called all of his direct reports to the meeting, and everybody came on board excited to meet this new CEO. And the very first question he asked of them in each of their business unit reviews was, What are customers telling you, and what are we doing to*

manage their experience? And of course, people were kind of dancing around the question because they truthfully didn't have an answer to it.

That moment gave people the trigger for the next time we have a business review or the next time I talk to the CEO, I damn sure better have a clear answer to this question. That question that he asked of all of his direct reports in that day sent the signal. They were measuring the experience, but nobody was paying attention, and it probably wasn't done very effectively. Their program shifted from a pet project to part of the company's DNA overnight.[57]

That's a powerful example of how a single question by the right leader can work to change the mindset of a company. Imagine, then, how the people who were asked that question passed on that way of thinking to their direct reports, and so on. The cascade effect can have a dramatic impact.

Leadership and Empathy

And of course, it's not just all about what leaders *say*. It is also about empathizing with the teams that need to do the work. What we're discussing in this book is large-scale change. Many call it digital transformation or business transformation because it requires fundamental changes often in short succession or all at once. This can be tough on the teams that work day-to-day and are suddenly told they must change the way they do all or part of their jobs.

I talked about this topic of leadership and empathy with Leon Gilbert, Senior Vice President and General Manager at Unisys. Here's what he had to say:

You can have the greatest strategy in the world, but if you're not thinking about organizational change management, these scenarios can fall apart, and especially around adult learning. We as adults, you know, we all learn at a different speed. We all learn in a different way, and we all want to consume things differently. And I think what's incredibly important as organizations think about organizational change management. . . Give choice to the employees, but also realize that not one size fits all. And it's very important that employee A and employee B have a different way of learning and different way of understanding and different technical capability, or a different whatever capability. But I think it's incredibly important that all major programs really focus on organizational change management.

There are many methodologies to this, but what is crucial, is executive sponsorship. It always needs to have that key level of executive sponsorship to help drive it. We don't just, in business life, just suddenly all decide to do something differently the following day. Technology can be there as an enabler, but unless we know about it, we don't necessarily use it. We assume people can just do things, and I think that's where organizational change management helps bridge that assumption.[58]

Onboarding and Training

Leadership also needs to ensure that employees are given the opportunity to be trained on what's expected of them. Too often, poor onboarding and training practices lead to employees failing to engage. They may even quit shortly after being hired.

Great leaders understand this and go beyond the perfunctory "first few weeks" of work where employees are bombarded with videos and training, then left to sink or swim. When I interviewed Steve Petruk, President of Global Outsourcing at CGS, a leading technology firm, he had this to say:

> *We need to empower employees. And to empower somebody is not enough. You also have to enable. For example, in the field service, ineffective training can be frustrating for an employee if they maybe haven't had the robust training they might have had when they were in a brick-and-mortar. And that's reflected in how they handle the call. It can even put them in an unsafe environment, and it provides less than a quality customer experience when it comes to solutioning those issues.*[59]

Chik-fil-A is a great example of the power of employee training as a key part of a customer experience program. If you have ever walked into a Chik-fil-A restaurant and interacted with its employees, you notice that there is a different approach to making a connection with customers. They say "please," "thank you," and "my pleasure" to their customers. They also endeavor to use customers' names when speaking to them. What are some of the effects of this training? They dominate the American Customer Satisfaction Index's ratings for fast-food chains, having topped the list eight years in a row.[60][61] Although there are many factors that contribute to this brand's ratings, consistent employee engagement and training are foundational to their efforts.

When and How Work Gets Done

Finally, I'd like to acknowledge the seismic shift the COVID-19 pandemic forced on the global workforce. Although many might have been part of global teams and done some remote work prior to the pandemic, the sudden changes brought about in 2020 accelerated brands' need for digital maturity in some ways and set back their CX in others.

As companies shift to "returning to the office," 63% of high-growth companies had already enabled work-from-anywhere models. As of mid-2021, 83% of workers surveyed by Accenture said that a hybrid model would be ideal.[62] A survey by Envoy in January 2022 said 63% of employees said flexibility in where they worked would make them feel more empowered in their jobs. Seventy-seven percent said their workplace had a hybrid work policy, with 8% saying there was either no policy or that work was fully remote.[63]

Time will tell what is truly needed to achieve and maintain success, but it's safe to say that we're not going back to the old way of doing business.

A customer-first, employee-driven approach takes many pieces working together, from having a clear picture of what *customer-first* means to tools to enable employees to serve customers in the best ways possible and find purpose in their work. Leadership must walk the talk and empathetically respond to employees that support the changes needed to move in the right direction.

2.0.2 Building an Innovation Culture

Just as corporate branding strives to unify a team by providing a shared vocabulary regarding a company's mission, vision, and values, a culture of innovation must be built on a shared understanding of what *innovation* means.

These semantics are important because a shared understanding helps employees orient their role in a company's digital transformation toward a North Star and embrace innovation within their role. Compare this to the distinction George S. Day made between Innovation ("big *I*") and innovations ("little *i*")—the former being widescale, disruptive change, and the latter being incremental improvements to existing products, services, and processes.[64]

Although the two can exist in the same company, it is important for a company to define not only where they are headed, but also what kinds of ideas are valued, the inventions that are sought, and the speed at which they want to get there.

In this chapter, we're going to look at what an innovation culture embraces and how to become more innovative as an organization.

Embracing Experimentation and the Possibility of Failure

First, we need to reframe our expectations of perfection. As I said in *The Agile Consumer* (2019), perfection is at most a specific point in time—if it can even be achieved. Although we should never stop striving for perfection, we need to understand that continuous improvement and achievement provide more sustainable business results than being "right" once. Look at the companies that were "right" at one point, then failed to hold on to that place of near perfection. If you need reminding, read up on any of these companies: Blockbuster Video, Polaroid, Kodak, Pets.com, Pan Am, and Compaq.

For a variety of reasons, one major factor of failure is risk aversion by leadership. According to a report based on a survey by London Research, of over three hundred client-side business leaders in spring 2022, "In a rapidly changing world, fear of failure and lack of support from leadership may be hampering organizations' capability to experiment."[65]

Forty-one percent of those surveyed in the report said that one barrier to being more adaptive is that their organization takes minimal risks. How do organizations look at this in a way that doesn't feel so threatening?

You change this behavior by openly embracing the idea that continuous improvement requires continuous testing, and not every test comes back with perfect results. When I interviewed Alex Atzberger, CEO of leading Digital Experience Platform Optimizely, about this need for leaders and teams to embrace experimentation, here is what he had to say:

> *Experimentation is ultimately all about observing your customer behavior and seeing what works and what doesn't work, and then moving more of your customers toward a solution that works.*
>
> *While you do this, you obviously have experiments that work out, and you have experiments that fail.*
>
> *You need to take the words failure and failing and put them into a completely different context of learning. How do you learn about things? You test things out, and if they don't work, you move on to the next thing. But you have now just avoided spending a lot of money and effort on something that didn't work. I've had conversations with customers who told me how elaborately they had done certain tests, and they failed—and they were ecstatic that they failed.*
>
> *Companies need to think more about this notion of learning and how you can understand your customer behaviors better by testing and experimenting rather than seeing it as a risk that you are taking for the business.*[66]

We've heard a lot of talk from startup culture in the vein of Facebook's (now Meta's) internal motto: "move fast and break things."[67] Although there may be rules about what's acceptable to "break," a culture that demands perfection in every idea and tactic is going to have an impossible time innovating fast enough to keep up with the competition.

Collaboration Is Key

Hand in hand with a culture of experimentation is one of collaboration. When I interviewed Judy Bloch, Principal CX Advisor at Medallia, about collaboration's role in making changes happen, she had the following to say:

> You have to drive change by influencing others. So, my piece of advice, whether we're talking B2B or B2C, is around building relationships. Look for others that are subject-matter experts in different areas of the business, and actively reach out—raise your hand. Get up from your desk, and look around see who else might have information to help diagnose the problem you're trying to solve. Then collaborate and work on it together.[68]

I'll come back to this later with some ideas for collaboration frameworks that can help drive this work across teams and departments in your organization.

Leadership's Role in Demanding Perfection and Supporting Change

True change, whether cultural, innovative, or anything else, takes leadership. Leadership's role is to set clear, measurable goals and to support their team as the transformation initiative hits snags, needs decisive action, or needs to pivot to best reach objectives.

First, leadership needs to make it fundamentally acceptable to make mistakes as long as those mistakes provide learning opportunities. Until employees are empowered to fail, innovation will be slower, and learning will not be shared among teams or within the organization. Failing to support mistakes puts a stranglehold on innovation.

Second, leadership needs to support the idea that, just like perfection, change is not something that happens once and is done.

Change is, and should be, the norm from now on. How change is managed is what separates a successful organization from one that struggles to innovate.

Leaders should also be ready to manage disconnects in expectation. In a recent survey by London Research of more than three hundred client-side business respondents, only 45% believed digital transformation involves fundamental organizational change.[69] In my experience, this is simply untrue and, quite frankly, a bit concerning. People, processes, and platforms go together. When they change, *all* these elements change, and that means organizational change is happening.

That said, in the same report, more than two-thirds of respondents indicated that they no longer use the term *transformation*. Instead they see their organization and the work performed as "constantly evolving, iterating, and embracing change." This makes sense and goes along with the idea of incorporating continual change into the culture.

Regardless of the words used, there needs to be tangible support from leadership to ensure the success of any digital transformation. After all, if executives aren't in favor of change or aren't excited about its progress, how can employees feel differently?

Finally, leaders need to *listen* to their employees and do something with the feedback that they receive. According to recent research, 56% of employees say their company rarely (once or twice a year) solicits feedback on their employee experience,[70] and even more (64%) say their company rarely acts on the feedback they do solicit.[71] It is estimated that the cost of this disengagement on the job amounts to $550 billion a year for US employers.[72]

This doesn't mean that leaders need to react to every idea or complaint, but it does mean that employees need to feel their feedback is going somewhere.

Organizational Culture

We should also consider the organization as a whole, not just individual employees and leaders. You can think of a company as a living system with individuals who work together to change the whole.

I like how Tim Brackney, President and COO of RGP, a global consulting firm that works with some of the world's leading brands, defined it when I interviewed him for *The Agile Brand* podcast:

> Company culture is the soul of the company. It's a defined way that people behave in an organization, and it's like a patchwork quilt of shared beliefs and values. For us, and I think in any culture, I think there are a few things that I think make a good company culture.
>
> I use two terms: clarity and transparency. They're similar words but have very different meanings in this context. Clarity, meaning that everybody's sort of beating to the same drumbeat. They know what the purpose of the company is and what our mission is every day. Then, transparency is to know how we are matched against the purpose that we've stated for our company. There are obviously several other things that make a great company culture, but for me, those things really help, particularly in a world where you're working both on-site and remote.[73]

So, organizational culture consists of both how individuals behave on their own, as well as how they interact with one another and get work done. It's important to understand that these two levels must coexist, and one can't obscure the other.

Similar to getting leadership buy-in, a digital transformation isn't going to be successful in the long term without a culture that can adapt and work together to drive the changes necessary. This is important to consider so you can head off potential issues.

I spend much more time discussing organizational culture in *The Center of Experience*, but I think it is important that we review a few relevant concepts. Let's look at a few aspects that are directly related to our innovation culture.

Competing Values Framework (CVF)

Originally developed from research conducted by faculty members at the University of Michigan who sought to identify organizational effectiveness in the early 1980s, the Competing Values Framework (CVF) has since been refined and validated by many third-party sources.[74]

There are a few appealing elements to this way of looking at organizational culture, which I will summarize briefly. Here are a few reasons why I believe the CFV is worth considering as a measurement framework:

- It operates on the premise that there is not a "good" or "bad" culture (other than an unhealthy one) and that an organization's culture may need to shift over time to achieve strategic objectives.
- It supposes that an organization does not just have one monolithic culture, but that an organization's culture is made of several aspects, along with different focuses (internal and external, flexible and focused).

Competing Values Framework

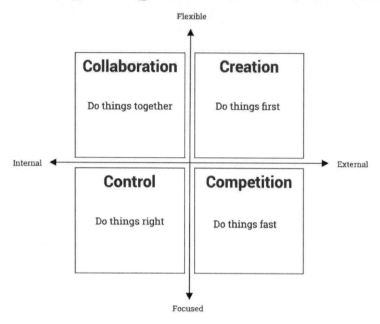

Figure 2.0.2.1, Competing Values Framework

As you can see from the figure above (Figure 2.0.2.1), the CVF contains four quadrants and two different scales of focus. To briefly summarize, there are two areas that are internally focused:
- Collaboration, which is teamwork focused
- Control, which focuses on operation and hierarchy

The two that are externally focused are
- Creation, which focuses on innovation
- Competition, which focuses on sales and growth

The quadrants on the top favor flexibility, and those along the bottom are more focused.

Understanding where your organization currently is in this quadrant, as well as where you'd like or need to be to accomplish your goals, can help provide a shared frame of reference for everyone.

Competing Values Framework

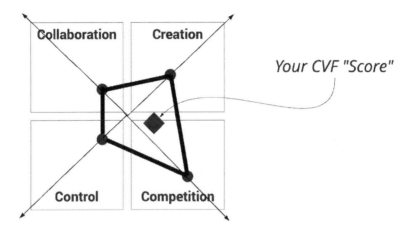

Figure 2.0.2.2, Plotting the results of the CVF assessment

As shown in the figure above (Figure 2.0.2.2), you can see where an organization sits in the quadrants when the results are plotted. Although it is rare that a score is zero, you will see that there is often a skew. In this case, you can see that the organization is generally externally focused (because the quadrants on the right are favored) and that there is a stronger focus on sales growth (because the Competition quadrant is favored).

I take this a step further in my other book, but more value can be gained if you plot the following distinct coordinates:

- Leadership's desired culture (based on a firm understanding of the organization's strategic needs)

- Employees' desired culture (based on the kind of company they would like to be working for)
- Employees' experienced culture (based on what the employees are currently experiencing in the organization)

Showing and measuring this disparity over time can help an organization close those gaps between where leadership needs the organization to go and where it currently is. Reviewing the company's CVF can also ensure that the current workforce is on board with the desired culture.

Absorption, or Absorptive Capacity

The second aspect of organizational culture is absorption, or absorptive capacity. According to researchers Susan J. Harrington and Tor Guimaraes, absorption is "the ability to recognize the value of new information, assimilate it, and apply it to commercial ends."[75] Plainly put, it is an organization's ability to incorporate new knowledge, change processes, and generally transform itself both initially and continually.

This concept is based on a few principles, including the following:
- Knowledgeable leadership is more capable of successfully leading their organizations in change initiatives.
- Better internal communication leads to higher success rates with change initiatives.
- Companies that value both an internal and external focus are most likely to have greater absorptive capacity.[76]

As we see in the figure below (Figure 2.0.2.3, originally featured in Harrington and Guimaraes's research) organizational culture translates to absorptive capacity, which leads to transformation success and, in the context of this book, to successfully adopting continual change when implementing a House of the Customer.

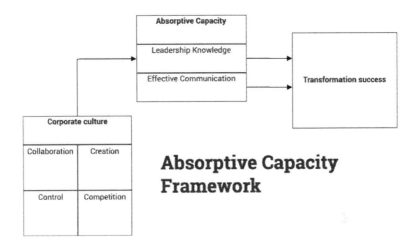

Figure 2.0.2.3, Absorptive Capacity Framework

Also, note the four items under "Corporate culture" in Figure 2.0.2.3. They are the same four quadrants we explored briefly in the section on the CVF. Harrington and Guimaraes's work on absorptive capacity utilized the CVF model to better describe the prime organizational culture for adoption and adaption to change:

In sum, organizations that emphasize the values of the group [as well as] developmental and rational culture dimensions should maximize their absorptive capacity. A culture strong in these three dimensions may lead to increased learning capacity and knowledge-sharing capability. Alternately, hierarchical cultures with their emphasis on stability and control are most likely to result in resistance to change and fewer receptors to the environment.

In layman's terms, there are a few ways to increase your organization's absorptive capacity:

- Increase leadership's knowledge and ability to articulate the need for change as well as what the change entails.
- Shift your company away from the Control quadrant, and more toward Collaboration, Competition, and Creation to set your organization up for more success with change initiatives.
- Improve the effectiveness of your internal communication channels and methods.

We're going to explore this last point a bit more in the next section.

Communicating Innovation

To understand more about how an innovation culture is created and grown from within, I interviewed Jon Ebert, Manager of North American Public and Industry Relations at John Deere. Although the company was founded in 1837, it continues to innovate and does so with a holistic approach that benefits internal and external audiences.

I asked Jon about this approach and about aspiring to be a brand where innovation and technology is valued. In addition, I asked whether such an approach could also be a North Star that helps attract talent that usually is drawn to more "traditional" tech giants like Google and Apple. I asked also him about the role storytelling and the brand play in that aspirational component. Here's what he said:

> *When you put a plan together and . . . focus on what your purpose is and [tell] that story to the right audience you've identified, what happens is you naturally have employees within your organization that see that storytelling. [They] buy into that culture [and] get excited and motivated by the work that's happening.*[77]

Jon went on to explain how John Deere exhibits at the Consumer Electronics Show (CES), a trade show known for its consumer product reveals of the latest gadgets and trendy devices. Although attending this event might not be what the typical consumer thinks of as a straightforward choice for a 150-year-old company that makes farming equipment, John Deere thinks differently and understands that innovation takes many forms and that communicating innovation externally and internally is fundamental to sustaining that innovation culture:

> *This year [at CES], we did a press conference because we brought in some new news. We select about twenty folks within the organization that are spokespersons that help us get that message out at CES. When you see those stories come to life in the engagements that we do with anyone, from a social media influencer to being featured in an article or a media interview, we talk about it internally. We focus on bringing the show back to our internal employees just as much as we focus on getting that narrative out externally. So we collaborate with a communications team internally, and we do stand-ups for internal employees. And you can see the excitement and the engagement from our internal employee base. That goes a long way toward building a culture that's motivated and inspired because they know that the work they're doing every day connects back to some higher purpose.*

Although your organization may not be at the top of the maturity curve, don't let that hold you back. *The Technology Fallacy* (2019) by Gerald C. Kane and others puts forth the idea that employee perception of digital maturity can have a strong impact on a culture of innovation.[78] Although perception only goes so far, it can be the difference between an unmotivated group of employees and one that is open to new ideas despite potential setbacks along the way.

Moving on from the foundation of our house, we're going to take a look at the business drivers that ensure our House of the Customer is aligned with our organization's strategic objectives.

2.1 Pillar 1: Business Drivers

*It is not the beauty of the building you should look at:
it's the construction of the foundation that will stand the test of time.*
—David Allen Coe

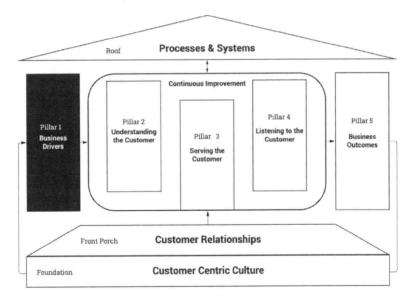

Figure 2.1.1, Pillar 1: Business Drivers

There are some obvious goals that most businesses want to achieve. More revenue, more profits, more customers, greater customer loyalty, increased spend per customer, improved customer satisfaction, and many other things. Yet stated business goals and what gets prioritized and invested in can leave critical gaps.

As an example, consider a recent Zendesk report, which found that 75% of enterprise leaders in North America agree that excellent customer service is a critical business priority, yet only 34% say that they're adequately investing in initiatives that support this.[79]

The business driver pillar is important because it is the "beginning" of creating value for both the customer and the business itself. What gets prioritized, implemented, and sustained over time is what ultimately determines several important things:

- The success of the business
- The customer experience and customers' satisfaction
- The strategic position of the business for future growth

North Star State

Business drivers are in their ideal state when the organization has the following in place:

- Clear goals and objectives that everyone from leadership to interns understands
- A systematic method to prioritize both strategic and tactical initiatives that is self-sustaining
- Processes and channels to communicate changes as well as the *need* for change throughout the organization

Our North Star state for business drivers includes a common understanding among executives, stakeholders, leaders, managers, and employees about what drives business value and how that value is defined. Although the level of detail may be different at the executive level than at the entry-level employee level, everyone shares a common vocabulary for business value in the ideal state.

To help steer you toward this North Star, I've provided two tools as part of this book. The first is a business value calculator that accounts for the elements of the House of the Customer and assists in calculating the business value of key initiatives. This business value calculator will help teams within an organization more easily articulate and understand how business value is defined and see firsthand the forces that can shape it.

The second is an initiative-prioritization model that allows us to take stock of all the items in our queue and rank them accordingly. Similar to the business value calculator, this makes the concept of business value more concrete through practical examples. I'll be discussing both in more depth as the book progresses. They're also both available in the appendix and for download from the book website.

Let's get started!

2.1.1 Business Value

Business Value

Figure 2.1.1.1, Business Value

Anyone from an agile background like myself has heard the term *business value* used to prioritize work in a sprint. Even those that don't have that background have certainly run across the term, which is often given different meanings. So what exactly is business value?

Simply put, business value is the ROI that is achieved by an initiative. But determining that value is more difficult than it might seem. Although it may be easy to define as seen in the figure below, it is often much harder to quantify.

$$ROI = \frac{Benefits - Costs}{Costs}$$

Figure 2.1.1.2, Calculating Return on Investment (ROI)

With competing external and internal priorities, the modern enterprise must strike a careful balance. This can make it hard to prioritize what should get done first and how to make sense of what drives the most ROI.

Benefit to Business

The first category we will discuss is the benefit to the business itself. By this I mean the financial, operational, and strategic importance that the initiative will play in improving enterprise performance.

Tangible Benefits

Tangible business value consists of all the things we can quantify and is often related to revenue and costs. Tangible business value always has a direct impact on the bottom line, however.

A positive aspect of tangible business benefits is that they are often relatively easy to measure and compare in a prioritization exercise.

Tangible
• Revenue Growth • Lost Revenue • Increased/Decreased Expenses • Return on Investment (ROI) • Cycle Time Reduction • Conversion Rates • Customer Retention • Percentage of Market Share • Decreased Work Effort • Sprint Velocity

Intangible Benefits

On the other hand, intangible business value includes things that may not have as direct an impact on the bottom line or may be more difficult to measure.

The challenge with intangible business benefits is that they are more difficult to give them a quantifiable value. That said, these measures can be extremely beneficial to improve.

Intangible

- Brand Reputation
- Positive/Negative Customer Sentiment
- Net Promoter Score
- Employee Satisfaction
- Analytics Reliability
- Campaign Bugs/Issues
- Legal and Contractual Compliance
- Regulatory Compliance
- Risk Avoidance or Mitigation
- Reduced Resources

Benefit to the Customer

The next category of business value is the benefit that an initiative provides to the end customer.

Customers are willing to pay for a more personalized experience. In the recent "Customer Experience Trends Report 2022," Zendesk found that a whopping 90% of consumers value personalization so much that they would spend more to receive it.[80]

Three Category Method

Although there are many ways to measure the benefit to the customer, the first method I recommend is using three main subcategories, which we'll discuss in turn.

Customer Satisfaction and Engagement

Companies use a variety of metrics to measure customer engagement, satisfaction, or similar factors. These measurements include net promoter score (NPS), customer satisfaction (CSAT), customer effort score (CES), and others, including proprietary scores. Many times, different parts of a business will measure several of these for different reasons, or they'll compile their own measurements for specific uses.

Although you may use a different set of measurements, a good way to prioritize your initiatives is by estimating the impact they will have on their engagement or satisfaction. These are likely to drive repeat purchases, recommendations, and cross-purchasing behavior.

Customer Education

The next subcategory is a measurement of whether the initiative will educate customers on the challenges your product or service addresses. The premise here is that a more educated customer is one that is likely to continue using the product, be more satisfied, and upgrade services.

Service or Product Adoption

The third and final subcategory is a measure of whether the initiative will generate greater adoption of the product or service it is intended to promote. This category assumes that greater adoption will provide more revenue, word of mouth, and opportunities to cross-sell other products and services.

Prioritization and determining business value should be easier when looking at the benefit to customer using this three-category method.

An Alternative: Customer Benefits Pyramid

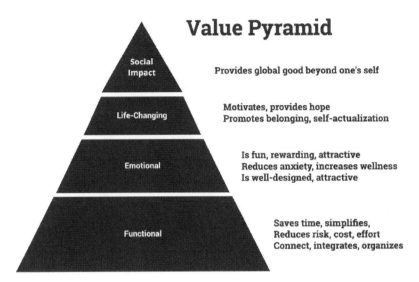

Figure 2.1.1.3, Business Value Pyramid

A different way to look at business value is to use the Business Value Pyramid (Figure 2.1.1.4). In this approach, we start with basic functional benefits and build toward more transformative values. Note that in this example we are looking at benefits in terms of the customer only, not in terms of the business. For this reason, this should be used in addition to other more financial and risk-oriented methods of measuring business value.

Starting at the bottom of the pyramid, we begin with the functional elements. These are things that save time, reduce risk, costs, or effort. They also include elements that connect, integrate, and organize things that a customer values more effectively.

In the next step in the pyramid, we have the emotional elements. These include things that are fun, rewarding, or attractive. They may also be things that reduce anxiety or increase wellness, as well as things that are well-designed and attractive.

The next focus is life-changing elements. These motivate and provide hope or promote belonging or self-actualization.

At the top of the customer benefits pyramid are items that transcend an individual customer and provide global or societal impact. Although not every product or decision can do this, determining this impact is still a good exercise for businesses to undertake.

Although I like this latter method, I tend to use the three-category method when quantifying benefits to customers, as the three categories are a bit easier to plug into prioritization models.

Cost to Implement

Cost to implement deals with a more direct financial component, including hard costs and fees. This includes the cost to produce and implement the initiative as well as measure the results. Many times, you will need to prioritize a pilot project or first iteration of an initiative, and this cost estimation can be critical in helping you decide the path forward. We can look at this business value in two subcategories, which we'll discuss now.

Internal Costs

The first subcategory is your internal resources, which include the employees and contractors that are part of the core team. In addition to costs such as salaries, you should take into account their hourly utilization and the cost of them focusing on the new initiative in relation to any existing roles and responsibilities.

External Costs

As you would imagine, this category consists of parties that are not employees or direct contractors of the company. This includes agencies, consulting firms, as well as fees for software platforms and licensed systems—essentially, anything that is not your internal human resources that also have a hard cost associated with them.

There are many factors that go into determining the business value of a proposed change or initiative. This ranges from benefits to the customer and business as well as the hard costs associated with implementation. Understanding these factors and weighing them meaningfully in prioritization is the next step after being able to calculate business value.

Calculating Business Value

To make true use of business value, we need some type of way to calculate it. For this, we will use a formula for business value realization that is straightforward yet flexible enough to fit into a slightly more complex model based on the House of the Customer.

Business Value Realization Formula

Let's explore the business value realization formula, originally introduced by Andrew Kaminski, and modified slightly for our purposes:[81]

The formula: $BV = aBV^1 + bBV^2 + cBV^3 - dBV^4$

Business Value $= BV$

BV^1, BV^2, and BV^n each represent different elements of business value (potential to generate revenue, increase customer retention, delivery efficiency, etc.), and a, b, c, and d are different levels of importance for each item. For instance, BV^1 may be more important to the business than BV^2; therefore, a would have a higher value.

We subtract the last item if this is a negative value. For instance, if there is risk to the organization, we might weigh that highly (i.e., d would be a high value) and subtract it since it is a negative value.

A House of the Customer–Specific Business Value Calculator

To help you with this, I've included a version of the Business Value Calculator in the appendix of this book as well as online. As with any of the tools I've created, feel free to make modifications for your own needs.

Communicating Business Value

Finally, it is important that business leaders communicate their definition of business value and ensure that there is a common understanding of what *done* really means.

I got a great definition of this in my interview with Sara Taheri of Prudential Financial Services for *The Agile Brand* podcast. Here's what she said:

> It's important that leaders set the business vision, the goals they want to achieve before selecting the technology that they think will be the silver bullet in solving their challenges. Having that business vision will make sure that whatever is being built keeps that North Star front of mind, whether that vision is to offer the fastest service, best healthcare, innovative tech—whatever that may be.

For example, if the business vision is to have the shortest, fastest, and most reliable quoting software out there, then this business vision needs to become the mantra and what every team member thinks about throughout the entire process as they are designing, building, and testing it. Every team member should keep asking themself, Are we building the right technology with the business vision in mind?[82]

We will discuss company culture, leadership's role, and even how to organize teams for new initiatives in more depth in the next section of the book.

Now that we've explored the business drivers and business value, let's explore the next pillar, which focuses on understanding the customer.

2.2 Pillar 2: Understanding the Customer

All truths are easy to understand once they are discovered; the point is to discover them.
—Galileo Galilei

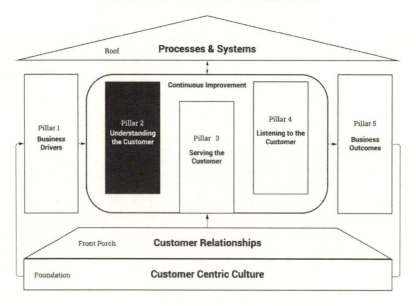

Figure 2.2.1, Pillar 2: Understanding the Customer

Although 98% of companies say that personalization increases customer engagement, and 83% of customers agree with them, only

48% of customers think that companies are doing a good job providing personalized experiences.[83] Closing the gap here starts with understanding the customer and how personalization can provide a better experience in the first place.

Over a third of marketers globally say that it is "very difficult" or "extremely difficult" to do any of the following: access data, achieve meaningful identity resolution for an individual customer, and have confidence in their data accuracy and quality.[84]

There also remains a question of whether to work with and improve existing data versus acquiring new data. In the CleverTouch "The State of Martech 2022" report, 72% of the 639 senior marketers across North America, Europe, and the UK responded by saying that they are inclined to spend resources on managing their existing data versus acquiring new data.[85]

Although our goal is to deliver personalized experiences that are valuable to both the business and the customer, we need to understand our customers before we can do that. To understand the customer we will need to listen to them.

North Star State

Our ideal, or North Star State, of listening to the customer includes our ability to accurately, and in real-time, collect valuable information about our customers that will help us provide the best possible customer experience over their customer lifetime. This data and information will ideally be stored and maintained directly by our organization (as opposed to third parties). The information will also include only what we need, and no more, because a big part of collecting data is also our governance and stewardship of that private information.

Thus, listening to our customers should enable the 1:1 omnichannel personalized experiences we need to deliver to stay competitive, but should not ask for more than we need.

What We Will Cover

In the next section on listening to the customer, we will discuss the key components of a first-party data strategy, including customer data platforms and their relationship to customer relationship management systems, or CRMs. We will also discuss the different categories of data needed to provide personalized customer experiences. Finally, we will look at the governance of customer data and what is needed for success.

Let's dive into our second pillar of the House of the Customer!

2.2.1 First-Party Data Strategy Components

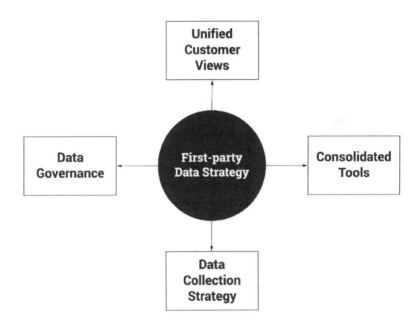

Figure 2.2.1.1, First-Party Data Strategy Components

Customers continue to demand a more personalized experience, going so far as to switch brands when they don't receive the level of service they expect. Although expectations from consumers are increasing, data privacy demands that eschew third-party data harvesting and identity stitching are also growing more complex. All of this adds up to brands needing to create a first-party data strategy that allows them to collect information directly from consumers and provide world-class customer experiences in return.

This realization is making its way across the business landscape as well. According to Nielsen's 2022 "Era of Alignment" report, nearly 70% of marketers believe first-party data is important for their strategies and campaigns.[86]

Let's review the key components of a first-party data strategy. Managing this well also sets your organization up for success amid growing customer expectations.

First-Party Data Collection Strategy

The first piece of our first-party data strategy is the approach to collecting data on customers. If you've been in marketing or customer experience for any amount of time, you know just how hard it can be to get customers to hand over even innocuous data. This usually happens when the customer doesn't see how sharing their data will benefit them, or they don't trust your brand will be a good steward of their information.

Customer Loyalty Programs

Although by no means a new approach, customer loyalty programs are still extremely effective at enabling brands to collect high-quality first-party data about their customers and their buying habits. In a survey performed by the Lacek Group and Sitecore in 2021, 66% of consumers surveyed worldwide said that not only have they signed up for a brand loyalty program, they know exactly how many brand loyalty programs they belong to.[87]

You've probably noticed that a lot more brands are getting into the loyalty program game. Getting more first-party data is a great reason to do this.

Subscription Business Models

You can probably see a theme here. In addition to customer loyalty programs, moving toward a subscription-based model has several advantages. In addition to financial benefits, a subscription model allows an organization to maintain a closer and more regular relationship with its customers, thus allowing them to collect more data about buying behaviors, preferences, and other activities to provide a more tailored experience. With more accurate data, businesses can provide value on a regular basis in the form of more personalized offers, content, service delivery, and product recommendations. Thus, customers are willing to share information to continue that relationship. It's a win-win for customers and businesses needing a robust first-party data strategy.

Brand Gardens

The term *brand garden* has popped recently and describes a "walled" area that a brand creates to attract and retain regular customers. In some cases, these brand gardens have valuable content, and in others, they may overlap with customer loyalty programs (by providing perks and incentives to members), or subscription business models.

I will give one caveat here. Although brand gardens can be effective for many, they are not a complete solution in themselves. Emodo's recent survey of C-level marketing executives shows that 64% of the respondents don't believe that brand gardens alone will solve their challenges obtaining customer data.

Alternatives

In the months ahead, media partners will be relied on more and more to think of "creative" solutions to third-party data challenges. In fact, in the Emodo report mentioned above, 84% of the marketing executives surveyed who were concerned about the lack of mobile device ID availability believed that media partners should offer privacy-compliant advertising solutions.

This means that brands and advertisers are looking to their partners to solve some of these first-party issues for them instead of allowing the entire challenge to fall on the brands themselves.

Unified View of the Customer

Delivering personalized customer experiences isn't possible if you don't have the data to support your view of the customer.

The second component of a first-party data strategy is a unified view of consumers. This includes knowing whether someone is a potential, current, or lapsed customer. By having a single holistic view of an individual customer, we can provide a better experience through personalization, automation, and tailored customer support. In almost all cases, this means the adoption of a customer data platform (CDP).

A CDP can be a single subscription-based cloud platform or a collection of purchased software products and custom-built data and reporting tools. The complexity of your CDP can reflect how broad your customer base is as well as how you communicate and interact with it. We're going to explore CDPs in more depth in the next couple of chapters.

Platform Consolidation

The third component of a first-party data strategy requires us to look at the platforms that are built to utilize the unified customer profile. With a CDP at the core, a solid first-party data strategy consolidates outdated or redundant platforms while enabling other advanced marketing tools like customer journey orchestration and next-best-action tools to provide a more personalized experience. Recent research by Medallia shows us that of 583 marketing and CX professionals surveyed around the world, 55% of organizations that identified as CX leaders were making investments in CDP in the next 12 months.[88]

When creating your first-party data strategy, evaluate the relationship between your customer relationship management (CRM) system, your marketing automation platforms, email providers, data management platform (DMP), and other systems. Most CDPs will easily integrate all of these, but it's not enough to have all the data flowing in one direction.

Instead, a first-party data strategy allows you to engage in personalized marketing and CX in new and expanded ways. Starting with unified customer profiles, you can then build toward a consolidated tool set of personalized marketing and communication platforms that deliver the type of tailored, dynamic experience your customers expect.

Customer Data Governance

Understanding how to utilize your customer data is key. However, consumers are increasingly aware of data privacy issues, which can prevent them from providing their information to brands they deem less trustworthy.

Data governance helps your organization manage the risk associated with collecting and storing your customer's data. Fragmented data poses risks, and inaccurate or incomplete data causes customer dissatisfaction.

I would like to quickly make the distinction between *ownership* and *governance*. Ownership is best handled by a smaller, focused team and involves the storage, security, and integrity of data. Governance relates to how data is shared, maintained, consumed, and normalized across business functions, systems, and processes.

In many cases, businesses may opt to use a content management platform (CMP), whose role is to keep track of opt-ins to communications as well as compliance with local or regional data privacy regulations or restrictions. The role of a consent management platform can be rather large, particularly at the enterprise level, though any organization operating globally should consider centralizing this role. There are many CMPs that can fit a wide range of needs.

The Data Privacy Concern Is Real

The processes involved in data governance can impact how a brand continues to earn its customers' trust. Remember, data privacy is not only a regulatory hurdle that demands compliance. Consumers are legitimately concerned about how their data will be used and accessed.

The number of data breaches continues to rise, with the Identity Resource Center's 2021 "Data Breach Report" showing 1,862 data breaches in 2021, surpassing the prior year's total (1,108), and even the previous record set in 2017 (1,506 data breaches).[89]

That is not even counting the "legitimate" uses of consumer data. According to a recent Coresight Research report, 96% of consumers surveyed were concerned about data protection and privacy, yet over one-third (36%) felt comfortable sharing data in exchange for a more personalized experience.[90]

A first-party data strategy requires planning how to collect customer data, how that data will be used to enhance the customer experience, and how your brand will earn the trust of consumers over time. By taking these three components into consideration, you can create a winning approach to the era of first-party marketing and customer experience.

In the next chapter, we're going to take a look at how to build a full-featured Customer Data Platform that builds off what we've learned about a first-party data strategy.

2.2.2 Building a Customer Data Platform

To deliver on a first-party data strategy, certain key components need to be implemented. One is a customer data platform (CDP), which is more than a single product. Although there are many cloud-based software products branded as CDPs, few have matured to have all the necessary features.

A CDP is a platform or collection of software that pulls data from multiple sources to create a single unified customer profile. This profile is then made available to internal systems for marketing and other purposes. One of the benefits of a CDP is that it sits outside of many internal systems and can collect customer and contact behaviors outside of internal channels.

That said, CDPs are a big priority for many organizations. In a recent study by Forrester on behalf of Zeta Global, 66% of the marketing, IT, and CX professionals surveyed stated that CDP is an important initiative within their organization.[91] The remainder of those surveyed acknowledged that their approach to customer data is more ad hoc and not part of the organization's strategic initiative. Sadly, those organizations are going to see an increasing gap in their ability to catch up with competitors who *do* see customer data as a key strategic priority.

Before we cover the technical details of what a holistic CDP should provide, let's first talk about what requirements a CDP have in order to be successful.

Acquiring Customers

The first category of requirements includes customer-acquisition methods, such as advertisements to reach anonymous customers by matching first-party cookies with email addresses when content is read, forms are submitted, or products and services are purchased. It also includes adding new audiences from second-party data sources to existing first-party data.

All of this adds up to the acquisition of new customers and a better understanding of previously unknown users across multiple touch points.

Engaging Customers

Next, we have requirements related to customer and business growth. This includes the definition and refinement of customer segments based on a multitude of criteria: spending level, types of products purchased, estimated lifetime value, browsing, searching behavior, and more.

Using this information, we can then personalize content across channels and drive customers toward the next best action that fits their needs and that of the brand.

Retaining Customers

Next, let's talk about customer retention. As we all know, it's a lot less expensive to keep existing customers than it is to acquire new ones. In fact, 57% of respondents from Forrester's April 2022 report said improved customer satisfaction was the expected result of having a modern, effective CDP solution (second only to higher revenue).

A CDP allows us to retarget customers across channels, provide better customer service through data and content sharing, and perform many other functions related to a strong customer retention strategy.

Optimizing Customer Relationships

Finally, a CDP should optimize not only your marketing and sales efforts, but your customer relationships and the experience you provide as well. This consists of tying marketing, sales, and customer analytics together to provide customers with offers, incentives, and next best actions by using a comprehensive set of data. This also supports ongoing optimization and continuous improvement over time.

Now that we've reviewed what a CDP should do for us, let's explore the components of a CDP. Remember, this may be a single software service that you subscribe to or several components you integrate.

Customer Data Platform Components

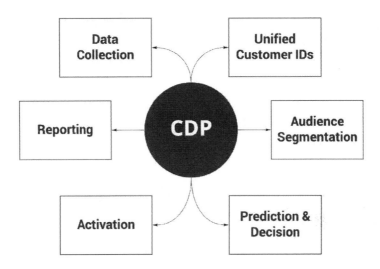

Figure 2.2.2.1, Components of a Customer Data Platform (CDP)

We've discussed the critical role that a CDP plays in creating personalized experiences. But how do you choose the right one with the features you need to fulfill the promise of the House of the Customer? Although the term CDP is used frequently, there are many different features that these platforms utilize (Figure 2.2.2.1).

It is also important to note that because of these varying definitions of CDP, buyers of CPDs can also be left dissatisfied with a platform purchased off the shelf. In fact, a Forrester report commissioned by Zeta Global in April 2022 interviewed 313 CDP users in marketing, IT, and CX and found that only 10% of CDP owners felt their CDP met all their needs.[92] It gets worse: only 1% of the respondents believed that their CDP would meet their future needs.

I like to define a CDP as a set of features and functionality that encompass five key areas:
1. Unified customer IDs
2. Audience and customer segmentation
3. Analysis and recommendations
4. Analytics and reporting
5. Customer activation

A few customer data platforms have strong capabilities across all these areas, though most are focused on a narrow feature set. Therefore, products that are branded as CDPs may not offer all the features we discuss below.

Unified Customer IDs

The first component we'll discuss is arguably one of the most talked-about features. In fact, in Forrester's April 2022 survey of marketing, IT, and CX professionals, customer identification was the primary function (64%) among participants of their current CDP; the second (59%) was ingesting data from various systems, which is closely related to this concept of a unified customer ID.[93]

With so many different marketing and data platforms being used, one of the biggest challenges that CPDs are expected to solve is unifying all third-, first-, and zero-party data (information proactively provided by a customer) in a single profile with a shared identification number or code. In fact, CommerceNext's 2022 survey of 114 online retailers revealed the process of data management ranked among the top challenges businesses face. Sixty-five percent of respondents experienced this challenge in 2022, up from 54% in 2021, indicating that this is a growing concern.[94] Interestingly, the top concern of the previous year was data *collection*; 63% of respondents indicated this was a top challenge in 2021, while in 2022, the data collection concern decreased to 47% of respondents. In other words, data collection and data management flip-flopped between the years 2021 and 2022.

With unified customer data in place, your CDP becomes your system of keeping track of customer profiles based on data gathered at all customer touch points. A CDP should also be able to deduplicate both known (individual customers who you already have a customer ID for) and pseudonymous users (individual customers that you haven't yet associated with a name or personal information). Getting this unified customer ID is a great reason to invest in a CDP.

Audience and Customer Segmentation

The next component of a CDP is enabled once you have unified customer IDs. Although direct, one-to-one personalization and communication is our North Star, good old-fashioned audience segmentation is still a valuable way to use your CDP. This is particularly true while building toward that ideal state. Your CDP should have a way to suggest new audience segments based on new insights while also working with ones you've predefined. Some platforms vary in flexibility in those two scenarios. "Building target segments" was the third-most-common answer in the Forrester report on CDPs, with 57% of respondents listing it as a primary function of their CDPs.

A CDP should be your system of record for both individual customer records as well as audience segments, and the goal should be a seamless, consistent experience for your customers. In many organizations, segments used for email marketing may differ from those used in advertising and retargeting. When there's often overlap, inconsistency means that you aren't offering a truly seamless experience for the customer.

Integrating your CDP with your CRM database, email service provider, DMP, and other platforms means that audience segmentation will provide the best and most effective user experience across multiple channels.

Customer Analysis and Recommendations

This brings us to the question of what to do with all those unified customer IDs and standardized audience segments.

Your CDP should be able to take customer data and audience segments and provide an analysis of behavior by channel, segment, and stage of the customer journey. This analysis can then be used to provide recommendations for content personalization opportunities, display next best offers or actions, or automatically trigger follow-up communications.

Some CDPs place more emphasis on profile unification and segmentation than on analysis and recommendations. That said, most provide at least some usable information to help determine what approaches may help engage customers and personalize their experiences.

Analytics and Reporting

With a CDP providing analysis and recommendations, the platform needs a way to share its data to be most useful. CDPs are not sold as analytics and reporting tools per se, so their ability to provide the following is often limited:

- Performance of audience segments
- Customer journey metrics

- Personalized content and offer performance

Although most CDPs don't put reporting at the forefront, their customers are seeking more features in that vein. In the April 2022 Forrester report, 63% of respondents said the most important CDP capability is providing unified dashboarding.[95]

Customer Activation

Our last category probably has the most variance between CDP platforms. Activation provides marketing channels with content and actions to implement the next best offer, action, or set of personalized content based on individual or audience segment behavior.

Although some have more robust features, others focus on analyzing customers and segments without triggering actions. For this reason, it's necessary to integrate with tools that support the following:

- Multivariate or A/B testing
- Content personalization
- Customer journey orchestration
- Integration of a next best action or offer, sometimes referred to as real-time interaction management

Although your CDP may not natively support the activation component, it's essential to integrate the right systems and take advantage of the benefits your CDP provides.

There are several criteria to consider as you choose a CDP or integrate multiple systems together. Some of the components mentioned earlier may be of higher priority than others. Additionally, some may be fulfilled by other systems. Other categories may require particular integrations that a specific CDP vendor cannot reasonably allow.

What if you don't have a CDP but already have a CRM system? Let's explore the differences.

What about CRMs?

If your main experience with customer data is with a CRM, you may be wondering how a CDP differs from a CRM. For those less familiar with the distinctions, let's briefly define them before we talk about how they can work together.

A CRM is a platform that stores current and potential customer information that allows an organization to identify potential sales opportunities, manage its marketing efforts, and more. It functions as a database that teams can bolster with external data sources, though not nearly as robustly as a CDP can. In addition to serving sales and marketing teams, CRM systems also serve customer service and technical support. Effective use of these platforms throughout the customer lifecycle can also lead to greater customer lifetime value.

Keep in mind that not every CDP or CRM falls rigidly into their given definitions, with some offering features or characteristics of the other. Although the CRM category is not new at all, the CDP category is still evolving into a core set of features. In the meantime, let's look at how an organization can use these tools together to offer a more optimal customer experience.

CDP = Customer Data System of Record

One of the greatest values of good data is that it can provide an objective source of truth. If an organization has multiple databases, customer records, and methods of gathering data, how can it identify that one source of accurate intelligence?

Because of the diverse information that CDPs collect and the way they use both structured and unstructured data to form a unified view, you can think of a CDP as your source of truth about an individual.

CRMs can benefit from this data through integrations, but the holistic view CDPs create puts them in a unique position in the data ecosystem. Likewise, CDPs benefit from integration with CRMs and other systems like DMPs.

Although a CDP and CRM can work well together, make sure that your teams understand what differentiates them, how each is kept up to date, and what information is best gleaned from each.

Different Teams Work with CDPs and CRMs Differently

Success depends on internal teams not only understanding the strengths and weaknesses of CDPs and CRMs in relation to their desired goals, but implementing best practices regarding how information is updated within each platform.

For instance, marketers can have great success with CDPs when running real-time marketing campaigns that benefit from an approach of personalization and next best actions. Because a CDP captures a mix of behavioral, transactional, and other data, it can build an accurate view of a customer that can be used to target that customer with relevant offers and information.

By the same token, sales professionals who are interested in building relationships with individuals will find a CRM more helpful than a CDP because of a CRM's ability to capture the information that is most beneficial to building one-on-one relationships. Relevant insights can be pulled out of a CDP and inserted into a CRM contact record, but many of the metrics that a CDP stores are difficult to act on. The volume of data collected with a CDP is easier for artificial intelligence and machine learning to parse than an individual person.

Although CDPs are helpful when building customer data profiles, don't forget that your internal sales teams use your CRM for critical business. This information can be incredibly timely and valuable. A solid understanding of the dynamic between CDPs and CRMs can help you see how to deploy each tool most effectively.

Understanding the CDP Market Segment

It is also important to understand that the CDP space is both quickly growing and somewhat immature compared to other spaces. Because of this, expectations of these platforms sometimes outpace reality.

For instance, in the same Forrester report where 57% of respondents identified building target segments as a primary function of their CDP, only 29% said they were "mostly satisfied" with the customer segmentation capabilities of their CDP.[96] There is some room for growth here!

This is not a reason to abandon investments in CDPs by any means. Instead, it is a caution to be realistic about what can be achieved with an off-the-shelf CDP. Other new or existing tools may be needed to augment tools in a rapidly maturing segment.

Data Clean Rooms

A data clean room is a secure digital environment where several parties can allow their first-party data to be combined and matched to generate better insights from campaigns and audiences. This serves a similar function as DMPs, which have historically relied on second- and third-party data sources to compile audience segments.

A data clean room allows multiple parties or businesses to collaborate without exposing individuals to third parties, thereby negating the need for a DMP. This, in theory, preserves consumers' privacy as well as the interests of the brands that share their data in the clean room.

Not only is this a viable option for many, but a 2021 Forrester Consulting survey found nearly one-third of global ad tech investment decision-makers indicated they either already or plan to use data clean rooms or similar tools with their first-party audiences.[97]

AppsFlyer, a company with a product in this category, states a data clean room enables app developers to securely join and produce insights based on their first-party data together with their marketing conversion data. As a result, app developers can accurately calculate and take informed actions on their marketing campaigns, thus increasing return on Investment while simultaneously preserving customer privacy.[98]

Expect to see more and more of these entering the market.

It is arguable that the tradeoff for customers is not so different from third-party data sharing, unless the sources and users of the data are equally trustworthy. That consideration notwithstanding, it seems to be a viable option for the industry to circumvent some of the challenges of a first-party-only approach.

Both CDPs and CRMs can play a vital role in the delivery of great CX. Although the landscape continues to shift as far as where a CDP ends and a CRM begins, understanding both and implementing the above approaches will lead you to greater success in your CX initiatives.

In the next chapter, we're going to look more deeply at the different types of data that we need to collect, manage, and utilize to provide the best personalized customer experiences possible.

2.2.3 The Data of Personalized Experiences

It would be impossible to understand personalization for an individual or an audience segment without collecting, categorizing, and understanding the multitude of data points available. This, combined with an understanding of *how* to apply the information, forms the basis of successful personalization.

If you feel your own organization's capabilities are not as robust as they should be when synthesizing data, you are not alone. In a 2022 study on the usage of customer data by Forrester Consulting, only 35% of marketers in enterprise organizations said they were "extremely advanced" in their usage of customer data for personalization.[99] To add to that, according to a recent report by analyst IDC, less than one-third of data practitioners (27%) completely trust the data that they have.[100]

A good way to start down the path to greater maturity is to categorize the data you use to personalize your customer experience. Let's begin here.

Personalization Data Categories

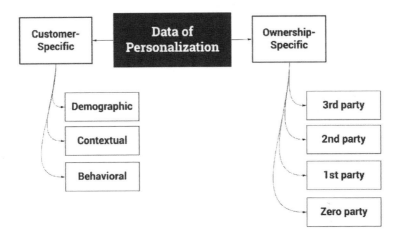

Figure 2.2.3.1, Data of Personalization

There are two main categories of customer data that drive personalized experiences (Figure 2.2.3), which are defined by how they relate to either the customer or the brand. These two categories can be defined as:

- Customer-specific
- Ownership-specific

Let's explore each category, as well as the types of data that are included in each below.

Category 1: Customer-Specific

This category is defined by its relationship to the customer and the way it can describe the individual. These categories are used to create audience segments from groups of individuals who share similarities.

Demographic Data

This subcategory consists of an array of applicable socioeconomic information, including but not limited to the following:

- Age
- Gender
- Ethnicity
- Income
- Employment status
- Home ownership
- Internet access

Contextual Data

This subcategory comprises information that provides perspective into a customer or their experience. Contextual data points include:

- Customer intent (e.g., why they are calling)
- Last item purchased (and date of last purchase)
- Personal information (e.g., name, email, address)
- Date of last customer service call (and if it was resolved or not)
- Time on hold
- Customer's preferred communication method
- Attitudes about your brand
- Last web page viewed
- Last email opened or received

To be most effective, contextual data needs multiple data points and touch points.

Behavioral Data

Behavioral data is data collected from a customer's interactions and engagements with your brand's many channels.

This can include events such as the following:
- Website or mobile app interactions
- Email sign-ups, opens, and clicks
- Subscription renewals
- In-store visits and purchases
- Customer service requests

Behavioral data is most useful when tied to a specific individual and the channel they use (e.g., website, mobile app, and call center)

Category 2: Ownership-Specific

The second category of personalization is determined by what entity is collecting, managing, and maintaining the data. It refers to the party that can claim ownership over it, whether that is the brand itself or a third party.

Note that there are bigger implications than simply defining ownership of data and the ease of access a brand has to the information. Customer data privacy is a major consideration here. For instance, while browser providers such as Apple, Microsoft, and (soon enough) Google plan to phase out third-party cookies by the end of 2023, 81% of companies say they have either complete or substantial dependence on them and that they would be seriously harmed by losing access.[101]

In the same set of research, 55% of organizations claimed to not be fully prepared for a world without third-party cookies. Meanwhile, 71% of companies predicted that the impending changes will lead to lower ROI on ad spend and a decreased ability to measure campaign efficiency.

Regardless of a brand's preparedness, 85% of consumers only want brands to make use of first-party data when providing personalized content and experiences. This means that brands need a plan to respond, and quickly.

Since we've been talking about third-party and first-party data, let's define the different types of ownership now. There are four subcategories, though there is overlap between some of them:
- Zero party
- First party
- Second party
- Third party

Zero-Party Data

We start with zero-party data. This is data that is "owned" by the brand and intentionally provided by the customer.

Forrester defines it as such:

> Data that a customer intentionally and voluntarily shares with a brand, usually in exchange for a benefit, such as an exclusive offer or reward. It can include preference center data, purchase intentions, personal context, and how the individual wants the brand to recognize them.[102]

Zero-party data can include information submitted in forms, survey answers, and other information provided explicitly by customers.

Zero-party data is often demographic, though specifically communicating intent could be considered behavioral. This is one area in which brands need to be concerned with the storage of personally identifiable information as well as ensure they are in compliance with regulations like the Health Insurance Portability and Accountability Act of 1996 (otherwise known as HIPAA).

First-Party Data

First-party data is data about your audience that you collect directly from their behaviors and interactions, not *from them* as in zero-party data. This data is often behavioral because it is collected as a customer takes actions like signing up for emails, purchasing products, clicking on ads or emails, or other trackable behaviors.

As the name suggests, first-party data is data that your brand owns because it is collected on properties that you govern and manage the data collection of. Although data collection and governance must follow local regulations and legislative requirements, first-party data (when collected according to those guidelines) can be used by your brand.

Second-Party Data

This category, as its numbering would suggest, falls somewhere between third-party data and first-party data, in that despite not owning it, you can use it within applicable regulations as long as you purchased or rented it legally.

Second-party data is essentially another organization's first-party data gathered directly from its audience. It may include data from activity on websites, apps, and social media, in-store purchase history, survey responses, and more.

Third-Party Data

Finally, third-party data is not directly collected or owned by your brand. It is data that an aggregator collects from various sources and sells as a package to augment an existing data set or stand on its own.

Third-party data may include anything from demographic data to contextual or behavioral data. Third-party data is used heavily in advertising segmentation and with DMPs.

Twilio's 2022 report (mentioned earlier) shows that over half of the companies surveyed are not prepared for a world where third-party data and cookies are unavailable. To make matters worse, over 40% of US internet users are already using browsers that block them, and even more users are utilizing browser add-ons and plug-ins that do the same.[103]

Looking Ahead: The Importance of Zero- and First-Party Data

Most marketers understand the importance of first- and zero-party data, and according to Forrester's recent report, 82% of them even have access to their zero-party data.[104] The challenge can often be in using that zero-party data effectively. Only 40% of those surveyed in the report claim to be effectively using their zero-party data to drive marketing success.

The good news is that, when presented with a good reason to do so, consumers are willing to opt in on communications. In fact, 81% of respondents to a survey from Lacek Group and Sitecore said that they have opted into brand communications recently.[105]

Although the deprecation of third-party cookies is causing a change in approach for marketers, publishers, and platform providers, it is not necessarily a bad thing. Let's discuss a few of these reasons.

Customers are generally not in favor of third-party data collection. It erodes trust in your brand and can even lead to bad experiences where third-party data doesn't match up with the individual. Because third-party data is often one step removed, there is a greater likelihood that it may not be a one-to-one match with the individual being targeted.

Additionally, from a brand perspective, this shift is forcing brands to rethink their data collection and improve their data quality. Publishers are in a similar situation, with an opportunity to create "brand gardens" and create their own equivalent of a DMP on a per-publication basis.

Finally, first-party data is not just better-quality data. Because you're the one collecting it, you have control over the methods, quality, and exact way it is used. A first-party data strategy means that you can design the collection of the data to include exactly what you need.

Connecting the power of first- or zero-party data to practical needs throughout the customer and marketing lifecycle does, however, remain challenging. According to Forrester's report, there are certain cases when zero-party data is used often—such as for retention and engagement with existing customers—while other cases such as acquisition don't utilize it as much.[106]

What Success Looks Like

It is important for brands to create a sustainable first-party data strategy to not only stay ahead of current data privacy trends but also deliver personalization effectively. This can also be referred to as a first-person data strategy.

Brands with effective first-party data strategies gain three main benefits:

- Better insights because they have a more direct understanding of individual customers
- More personalized experiences because their processes, platforms, and systems foster an improved customer journey, increased repeat purchase behavior, loyalty, and advocacy
- Compliance, because better customer data governance gives them greater control over privacy, consent, and compliance

Understanding customer-specific and ownership-specific types of data and how to effectively use each to engage with your customers requires coordination across several levels. These requirements include an understanding of your customers' behavior, integration between platforms and analytics, and an understanding of the regulations and legislation that applies to your data collection, storage, and usage.

This then brings us to how we must plan as brands to be good stewards of our customers' data.

2.2.4 Customer Data Governance

Thought by many to be the most important element in business today, data is the lifeblood of any company. Employees are vital but may come and go over time, which causes organizations that count on individuals for institutional knowledge to be at particular risk. Your company's information, when handled correctly, should last as long as it remains useful to the business.

Customer data governance, done well, impacts how your business can maintain and continually improve on CX. Although every organization has unique customer data needs and applications, one thing is certain: data governance is critical to the strategic growth, sustainability, and optimization of a company.

In this chapter, we're going to explore a few aspects of how customer data governance impacts an organization's ability to deliver personalized customer experiences.

Increasing the Speed to Impact

Good customer data governance minimizes the hurdles teams and customers go through to access useful information. This is often accompanied by or closely follows a digital transformation initiative, which may be required to connect data sources in the first place. Data governance is then needed to maintain all the work done to connect, standardize and analyze the collected information.

Collaboration Across Teams

Have you ever been in conversation with a colleague from another department and heard them say that *their* data says one thing, even if it contradicts your own?

This kind of disparity between siloed customer data gathered by departments or teams is one of the issues good data governance solves. Organizational data should be owned and accessed by everyone in the company that can benefit from using it. If there are different "versions" of the truth, then you're not going to be able to make good decisions or even have confidence that you've succeeded. No one will be able to agree when you've achieved goals because they will be looking at different statistics!

Customer data governance normalizes data sources. When done well, it also allows information across the organization to be analyzed without cumbersome data translation or transformation efforts. This means your teams are speaking the same language and can make intelligent decisions quicker.

Real-Time Optimization

When would you rather have a great customer experience: immediately, or the next time you interact with that same brand? It might seem obvious when asked that way, but many companies are stuck collecting data that impacts their decisions *after* a customer has had an experience.

I'm referring, of course, to survey scores like customer satisfaction (CSAT), net promoter score (NPS), or customer effort score (CES). Although these have their place in a successful CX measurement initiative, companies are missing out if they overlook real-time customer insights and journey orchestration.

Customer journey orchestration allows a brand to personalize a customer's experience in real-time by utilizing multisource data to decide what content and offers to show that individual. When done in a multichannel or omnichannel approach, data from many distinct platforms must be unified and integrated.

This is where good data governance comes into play. Even though many automation tasks may fall to a specific department, the data needed to optimize any of those experiences often come from platforms and teams that span the entire organization.

Good data governance helps unify these sources, processes, and systems and ensures that customers receive impactful personalization through a wide range of experiences.

As you can see, customer data governance can have a major influence on how the customer experience is delivered, measured, and enhanced. It can help teams work together better and help customers get more personalized service. All this adds up to a significant impact on any organization.

Customer Data Governance Principles

There are many benefits to strong customer data governance. This includes increased cost and time efficiency, risk mitigation, greater consistency, and more quality of data. Who should "own" data or contribute to data governance within an organization, however, varies greatly. Some companies have a department responsible for governance, while others have cross-disciplinary teams that handle it.

Data governance that restricts beneficial usage within an organization doesn't increase its value, and in many cases, it leads to inefficiencies and lost opportunities. Let's review four principles to keep in mind as you prepare your customer data governance practices.

Principle 1: Being a Steward of Your Customers' Data Is a Privilege

Data privacy and security are increasingly on consumers' minds. For instance, a recent survey by Frontier Communications of 1,001 consumers showed that the top two most desired additions to social media platforms are data privacy (61.4% of respondents) and more security features (54.1%). Consumers also showed interest in data transparency (47.8%). This far outpaces things like better content (22.4%) or other features.[107]

With so much resistance to personal data sharing, brands need to understand it is a *privilege* to keep and use customer data. Instead of taking data for granted, companies should consider data as granted to them and owned by their customers. We're lucky to have access to it.

Principle 2: Data Is an Asset of the Enterprise, Not a Specific Team

Who benefits from data in your organization? I bet your answer includes several different teams, disciplines, and roles. With so many team members within an organization benefitting from data, it should be considered an *enterprise* asset, and not a *team* asset.

A shared customer data governance model helps reinforce this idea of data being an enterprise-wide asset. This is because many participants across a diverse set of roles, capabilities, and teams can have input on how data is treated within the organization. This contrasts with marketing having ownership and governance over marketing data, sales over sales data, and so on.

This larger-scope view of enterprise data can give team members more context when working with customer data and help them better understand how their work connects with what other teams are doing. Having this context can provide a better understanding of how different parts of the organization work together, how customers interact and behave throughout the entire lifecycle, and more.

Principle 3: Agile Organizations Need Cross-Organizational Data

Does your sales team only benefit from sales data, or would information about your latest marketing efforts and customer support inquiries help them make better decisions? Having access to both leading and lagging data helps teams stay agile in a fast-moving environment. Access to real data helps teams avoid making the wrong decisions based on anecdotal information or incorrect hypotheses.

A shared customer data governance model helps organizations be more agile, make better decisions, and reduce the time and effort it takes to make important changes happen. One reason for this is that the quicker teams can access information, and the more diverse the sources of data within the organization, the better insights they can gain.

Principle 4: The Customer Benefits When Data Is Shared with Responsible Parties in the Enterprise

Remember, the *customer* is at the center of our considerations when building a House of the Customer. When they need to complete a transaction, does your customer care what department, division, or team they need to work with to solve their challenge? Furthermore, does that customer care about what internal system needs to be accessed in order to answer their question? I would venture to say that they don't. As long as your customer trusts your company with their data in the first place, they are not concerned with who in your organizational chart they need to talk with to solve their issue.

Let's look at this from the customer's perspective. How many times have you called a customer service line, only to have to give your account information two or even three times to different people that work for the same company? There may be a perfectly logical explanation, such as that their systems don't "speak" to one another, but how does that benefit your customers?

Research by Deloitte from 2020 states that 75% of consumers expect consistency in experience, but nearly 60% say they still feel like they're talking to a company with disconnected departments instead of a single unified brand.[108]

Although the example I provided is relatively simple, there are many areas where a lack of shared data either has an opportunity cost or provides a negative customer experience, both of which can end with less-than-stellar results. For instance, when your product and customer support teams don't see eye to eye, issues and solutions that might seem obvious to your customers are obscured because of unnecessary disconnects.

A shared customer data governance model helps because customers no longer have to navigate an organizational hierarchy they neither need nor want to understand just to get answers to a question. Instead, because data is governed on the back end, the customer can experience a more seamless experience on the front end.

As you can see, customer data governance impacts both internal and external audiences. Questions of ownership, data sharing between teams and departments, and the flow of data between systems can affect efficiency, customer satisfaction, and much more. Shared data governance can create a more agile organization that can anticipate and respond to continual change.

2.3 Pillar 3: Serving the Customer

We require from buildings two kinds of goodness: first, the doing their practical duty well: then that they be graceful and pleasing in doing it.
—John Ruskin

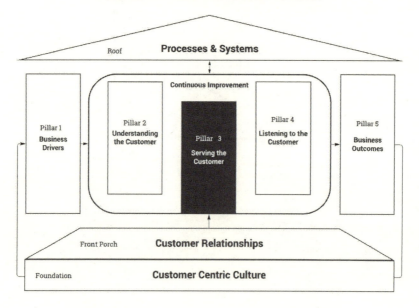

Figure 2.3.1, Pillar 3: Serving the Customer

We now come to the central pillar of our House of the Customer, where we will discuss how to utilize what we know about our customers to serve them the best. Much of what we talk about will cover digital content and experiences, and for good reason. For business-to-consumer (B2C) organizations, 53% of engagement is already digital, and these companies expect a 21% increase in digital customer engagement by 2025.[109] This means that half of engagement is still offline, or in real life (IRL), as some would say. This means that to best serve our customers, we need a strategy that provides a seamless experience in both online and offline worlds.

North Star State

The North Star state of this pillar is closely intertwined with one-to-one omnichannel personalization.

When we serve the customer effectively, we are achieving the goal of providing the right content or action, at the right time, on the right channel, to a customer that is ready and willing to engage with it.

Doing this well requires the elements we've already discussed (e.g., customer data) as well as a few pieces we have yet to cover. The ideal scenario is more than a reactive, trigger-based marketing messaging strategy; it's a proactive, next-best-action approach. This means we have a more strategic, customer-journey mindset focused on growing loyalty rather than tactical short-term marketing automation.

This means that we can adapt our messaging, the offers we provide, the channels we provide them on, and more based on the individual in real-time. To do this, we need to understand a lot about our customers and a lot about the content, offers, and experiences we can provide. That's where this pillar of serving the customer comes into play.

2.3.1 Defining Personalized Experience

The statistics supporting personalization and personalized experiences are clear. Ninety-one percent of consumers are more likely to shop with brands that provide relevant offers and recommendations,[110] and 80% of customers are more likely to purchase a product or service from a brand that provides personalized experiences.[111] What's more, 76% of consumers get frustrated when their experience and content are not personalized.[112]

But what exactly do we mean by *personalization*? I think Salesforce defines it well:

> *Personalization is the act of tailoring an experience or communication based on information a company has learned about an individual. Just like you may tailor a gift for a good friend, companies can tailor experiences or communications based on information they learn about their prospects and customers.*[113]

To further define this, let's look at some examples.

Email personalization is a great way to connect with customers, but this should extend beyond the subject line. If your business caters to many different clients, your organization must consider how to deliver the right message to the right user. This can be done by segmenting your email list by job function, company type, user demographics, and so on. However, the most effective way to deliver the right content is through personalization. Using machine learning, you can target users based on browsing history, geography, and location. This leads to more personalized results instead of guesses based on flat personas.

Increasing engagement is an important goal for marketers. Customers between their first and second purchases pose a higher risk of not making another one. You can mitigate this risk through personalized web pages that create a chance for your organization to connect with customers through dynamic content, recommended products, and updates based on location and weather.

Product Recommendations

Product recommendations are used in e-commerce and other industries in which algorithms analyze customer behavior. A user then sees related products, offers for specific product categories, or similar purchases by other users. This data is gathered in a variety of ways:

- Previous website sessions (pages visited)
- Technographic profile
- User-generated data (account settings, surveys, etc.)
- Behavioral targeting
- User-data-generated offers (e.g., birthday sales)
- Real-time data (e.g., geographic location, time, day)

Personalized Advertising: Targeted Ads

Another common method of targeting specific audience segments is through advertising. Although third-party-cookie deprecation will pose short-term challenges, advertisers, publishers, and DSPs are quickly moving toward solutions. Needless to say, digital advertising isn't going anywhere.

However, technology that blocks advertisements, or the data used to show targeted ads, could continue to hamper their effectiveness. Still, there does seem to be a growing trend toward openness to digital advertising in younger generations. For instance, a recent survey of 1,001 respondents showed that 56.6% of baby boomers perceived targeted ads as "annoying," while 41.4% called them "invasive." Generation Xers also shared those sentiments at a higher rate than millennials (43.9% and 31.6%) or Gen Zers (37.3% and 32.4%).[114]

Customer Service

You just *know* the difference between personalized and nonpersonalized customer service. For example, having to provide your name and account number to three different representatives is not receiving personalized customer service. The same is true when the representative assisting you doesn't have access to key details about your purchase or order history. They aren't empowered with the information to best help you.

Remember, great customer service doesn't *happen*. It is enabled by proper training, access to key customer details, and a process built around creating seamless experiences for the customer first.

In-Store, Frontline Retail, and Hospitality Experiences

Think personalized experience can only occur in the digital realm? Think again. Well-trained employees have been offering personalized experiences to customers for years. Think about a neighborhood restaurant with regular customers. Chances are, they don't need to order their favorite drink or dish after visiting several times.

Now take that same idea and augment it with customer data and history, and the frontline customer experience in retail, restaurants, and hospitality can be transformed. You can already see this when, for example, you're a rewards member at a major hotel chain and are automatically given a room on your preferred floor or are prompted for a late checkout option if that is available to you.

Dimensions of Personalized Experiences

Now that we've looked at a few examples of personalized experiences, let's take a look at the dimensions of personalization (Figure 2.3.2) that must be designed to achieve our North Star one-to-one omnichannel experience. To get there, however, we may take a few different approaches.

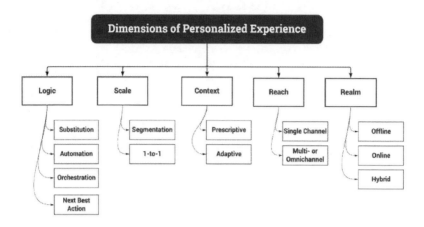

Figure 2.3.1.1 Dimensions of Personalized Experience

Logic

The first dimension we'll explore relates to *how* personalized experiences are delivered. The logic that drives personalization will also drive how the experience is delivered across channels and how personalized that experience is. Although each of these subcategories is a different type of logic, many are used in conjunction with one another.

Substitution

This first type of logic involves replacing a generic greeting with a customer's name or relevant information. For instance, if you were sending me an email, you might say "Dear Greg" instead of "Dear Valued Customer."

This is by far the simplest type of personalization available, yet it remains effective, particularly when used with other tactics. According to Campaign Monitor, marketers typically see a 20% increase in sales revenue from personalized email campaigns.[115]

Automation

Unlike substitution, automation is driven by action and occurs in reaction to something. This automation may be internally motivated (e.g., driven by an offer that a brand wants to send to a particular audience segment), or it may be externally motivated by the actions of a customer (e.g., signing up for an email list, downloading content, adding an item to an e-commerce shopping cart, or making a reservation).

In all of these cases, the systems and communications are often personalized using the substitution method above and automatically sent at the appropriate time, such as once a purchase completes.

It is important to note that automation generally deals with a single step or action, not a sequence of actions. It is very much based on a reaction to an action, and then the automation's "job" is complete.

Marketing automation is most helpful when your messages or responses require minimal personalization. This personalization might include readily available information, such as a customer's first and last name or recent product order. If the need to tailor the message or approach grows more complex or needs to utilize multiple channels, marketing automation may not be sophisticated enough.

Orchestration

Next, let's explore orchestration. This takes automation a few steps further because it "orchestrates" the experience across multiple channels. Although marketing automation may only include sending emails based on an action or trigger, customer journey orchestration may work across three or more channels that coordinate with one another.

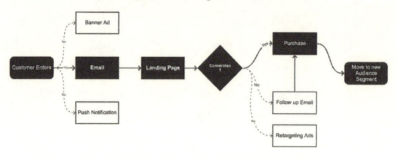

Figure 2.3.1.2, Customer Journey Orchestration

The figure above (Figure 2.3.1.2) maps out the customer journey from start to finish, with multiple steps and several decision trees along the way that can be automated depending on what a user does or doesn't do.

For instance, a visitor to a specific page on a website may stay for a few minutes and leave, but they signed up with their email address to download a white paper while they were there. Because of this, they are now shown a retargeting ad on social media, driving them back to the website for more information. One or two days later, they receive an email with a coupon code that drives them to a personalized landing page, where a deal is created. This example uses social media, email, and a personalized web experience.

Journey orchestration creates a seamless experience for the customer as opposed to a series of discrete, automated channel experiences. According to Braze's "2022 Global Customer Engagement Review," brands considered leaders in customer engagement were 25%

more likely to use a single solution to orchestrate their cross-channel campaigns and communications.[116]

Unlike automation, orchestration is concerned with sequential steps of actions and reactions. Customer journey orchestration provides a prescribed "journey" that a customer embarks on with starting and end points, with several decision points in between. Although customers may differ in some of their actions and channel preferences, orchestration is built on the idea that all or most customers of a certain type follow a similar path to get from one point to another.

A common orchestration pathway is driving a customer from initial awareness of a product or service to making a purchase. The touch points are orchestrated in a way that guides customers to education about the product and ultimately to a seamless purchase transaction.

Note that substitution and automation may also be utilized at several points in customer journey orchestration. In this case, orchestration could almost be considered additive.

Next Best Action

This brings us to the last method of logic—and perhaps the most unique. Unlike orchestration, next best action is less concerned with a predefined pathway for a customer. Instead, next best action, utilizing artificial intelligence and machine learning (AIML), determines the best content, offer, or action a customer should take to achieve the maximum outcome. This outcome can vary from what the business deems the most logical, or it could be based on the customer's changing needs.

Although this is easy enough to understand in theory, in practice this can be the most difficult approach for marketers, CX teams, and others to wrap their heads around. After all, in addition to creating multiple content variations to personalize experiences, next best action also dictates that the journey itself be more free-form. Although this may seem intimidating at first, next best action is a more customer-centric approach to logic. These systems combine AIML decision-making with rules-based logic so that some transparency remains.

I like the way that Shoel Perelman, VP of Product and 1:1 Customer Engagement Decisioning and AI at Pega described it when he was a guest on The Agile Brand podcast:

> *I think of it as the difference between starting with the product versus starting with the customer. In traditional campaign marketing, you usually you have a product and you're finding who can I talk to this who could I talk to about this product right. With next best action. It's kind of the opposite. It's the idea that you have a customer right now you have a precious moment with them. You could say one thing to them. You could start one conversation. What's it going to be? You don't want to squander that moment. So, the idea is that, with all the different things that you could talk about, they all have a little battle. And they duke it out for what is the right balance between what the customer is going to want to hear about, what will they care about, and what value will it generate for the business. That's really what I think next best action is is about and how it's different from kind of the traditional campaign approach.*

Next Best Action

Figure 2.3.1.3, Next Best Action

Although they always have an element of predefined orchestration, next-best-action journeys utilize AIML to map a customer's most likely actions related to business priorities. The next-best-action system uses scorecard models as well as predictive models based on similar customer behavior to determine the best messaging and platform for the individual for conversion. With next-best-action approaches, you are still in control of the outcomes you want, but your customers have more control over how they get there.

Rest assured, next best action offers the ability to weigh certain offers or actions over others if they become a bigger priority. The biggest benefit, however, is its ability to individualize the customer experience in a way that automation and orchestration are not flexible enough to offer.

The best choice between automation, orchestration, and next best action depends on your goals as well as your resources. There are many cases when an organization can use all three methods to provide an optimal customer experience. When and how you use marketing automation, customer journey orchestration, and next best action will also evolve over time as your needs mature and your customer expectations grow.

Next best action also aligns better with our North Star of creating the greatest customer lifetime value. When done correctly, the next best action should improve the customer experience while bringing maximum business value. This, in turn, should translate into findings and outcomes that can be applied in order to improve subsequent customer experiences.

Scale

The second category is defined by how granularly we personalize content, offers, and experiences, whether at a broad or individual level.

Segmentation

Segmentation requires identifying a subsegment of people within your larger audience. A good example would be targeting loyalty customers with tailored messaging. The aim is to produce better business outcomes by delivering more relevant experiences. In turn, this encourages the customer behavior you want.

One of the challenges of segmentation is that to produce greater outcomes, you have to target smaller and smaller segments. You will eventually hit a plateau where the spend to manage the segments is greater than the return. That said, segmentation-based personalization can produce substantial results if your segments are large enough and your experiences are tailored well enough.

One-to-One Personalization

The term *one-to-one personalization* refers to providing an optimal experience to an individual based on their unique relationship with the brand, such as order history, number of years as a customer, or prior experience with customer service.

One-to-one personalization doesn't always have to be for long-standing customers, however. Prospective customers can also receive personalized messaging based on their website visit history, geographic location, the type of device they use, and other factors that a brand can utilize.

Tools such as AIML can make one-to-one personalization even more effective because AIML can learn more about an individual's behavior and preferences over time. This can occur at the individual level and by comparing an individual to other similar customers.

Context

The third category of personalized experiences refers to the drivers or factors that cause personalization. We'll look at this using two primary lenses: prescriptive personalization and adaptive personalization.

Prescriptive Personalization

Prescriptive personalization means tailoring an experience with a customer based on preset rules or choices that a user has made. These business rules are most often tied to a particular audience segment, which helps guide the best and most appropriate personalized content, offers, and experiences.

Going deeper, we prescriptive personalization can be explicit or implicit. Explicit prescriptive personalization is based on what a brand already knows about the user through information they have provided and actions they have taken, while implicit prescriptive personalization is based on what can be assumed and extrapolated about the actions a customer has taken.

Adaptive Personalization

Adaptive personalization means that a current or potential customer's experience will evolve as they take a series of actions and as a brand begins to understand more about them.

Some of this adaptive personalization may utilize preset rules that trigger once more information is learned about the customer. This means adaptive personalization gives way to prescriptive personalization, and some of it may continue to adapt over time, utilizing next-best-action approaches. Adaptive personalization involves both predictions about what a customer may want as well as reactions to what they have already done or where they are in the moment.

What about Offline Interactions?

In our real-life interactions with customers, we need to rely on a little bit of each type of context. This means having processes and systems that provide both prescriptive and adaptive information available to frontline employees, customer service, and technical support representatives.

It also means that we need to train our employees how to utilize context in real time and *without* relying solely on platforms. Although we don't have enough space in this book to dive into this in more detail, this is where empathy, emotional intelligence, and other factors complement a robust onboarding and ongoing training program.

Reach

The fourth category, reach, refers to how broadly personalization is available across the customer experience. This is a metric of how many platforms and channels are working seamlessly together to provide a personalized experience, content, and offers.

Single Channel

The first and most basic category of reach is on a single channel, such as email or a website. Although doing personalization well is never easy, single-channel personalization offers tailored experiences in the simplest way possible.

Personalized content is favored by customers, but there can be backlash or frustration if only limited channels provide personalized content. Once the customer uses a different channel, their experience becomes disjointed, which can negatively impact their satisfaction.

Multichannel

Brands that engage in multichannel personalized experiences are going to see better results than single-channel experiences.

Although more difficult to achieve than single-channel personalization, multichannel personalization delivers the types of experiences that consumers expect.

Doing multichannel personalization well requires having shared audience segment and customer profile definitions across the organization. This involves coordinating CDPs, DMPs, CRMs, and other stores of customer information, activity, and behaviors.

Omnichannel

This brings us to our North Star goal of omnichannel personalized experiences. As we've discussed already, this means that *all* channels your brand provides, both online and offline, are coordinated to deliver consistent content, campaigns, offers, communication, and services.

Few organizations can claim to achieve this type of personalization, but this should remain the goal. It is possible to achieve some type of consistency at the very least. We'll talk more about how to work toward achieving that North Star goal in the next section of this book as well.

Realm

Our last category is the realm—where personalization occurs, whether online or offline (IRL).

Online

This one probably doesn't need a lot of explanation. Online refers to anything on the web, your mobile device, or your computer. It includes all the websites, mobile apps, chatbots, and online tools that you use to connect with brands, receive customer service, and have other brand experiences.

Of course, the online world continues to evolve and has room to expand into virtual reality and the Metaverse. As of the writing of this book, those areas are still in the hype phase. That will not always be the case, however.

Offline

We've been spending a lot of time discussing the digital realm and talking about digital experiences. Although there has been massive growth in the number of digital interactions—tripling from June 2017 to July 2020 from 20% to 60% globally (65% in the United States)—this still means that between 35% and 40% of customer interactions are still happening offline.[117]

It can be easy for those of us who work in online channels to assume customer interactions only need to be personalized in digital realms, but there are still so many opportunities for improvement in offline interactions. Perhaps this is one reason why, in Medallia Institute's 2022 report on CX best practices, 65% of organizations that identify as CX leaders are making high-priority investments in improving the consistency of customer support experiences.[118] Hospitality, travel, healthcare, and many other industries will always need to provide a seamless offline experience, though some of the big challenges facing brands come down to exactly how seamless their online and offline experiences become.

What about Augmented or Mixed Reality?

Augmented reality (AR) introduces an interesting hybrid between the online and offline worlds. As of the writing of this book, AR is slowly gaining traction in personalized experiences, and major technology companies are making strides to create beneficial AR experiences. As time goes on, I believe AR will play a major role in our experiences and truly "augment" our offline ones.

Now that we've explored the dimensions of personalized experiences, we're going to explore the infrastructure needed to deliver those experiences.

2.3.2 Infrastructure for Delivering Personalized Experiences

There are a lot of marketing technology platforms and related systems. A lot. According to MarTec's "Marketing Technology Landscape Supergraphic (2020)," there were a total of 8,000 martech solutions cataloged and categorized.[119] This was up 13.6% percent from the previous year, but even that number doesn't tell the whole story. Factoring in business acquisitions and mergers and platforms that were retired, the growth of new entries was around 24.5%. Yes, that means that nearly one quarter of the platforms on this 8,000-entry list didn't exist the year prior.

That's the long way of saying that there is a lot to keep up with. Fifty percent of marketers surveyed in CleverTouch's "The State of Martech 2022" report agree, saying that they are overwhelmed by the technology at their disposal.[120]

Additionally, according to a Forrester report for Tealium in 2019 that surveyed 330 customer intelligence leaders in the United States, United Kingdom, France, Germany, and Japan, there is much room for improvement regarding the technology supporting a personalized customer experience. On a four-point maturity scale, only 36% of respondents were considered "leaders" or "pioneers" in technology solutions, with 20% being considered "laggards."[121]

With nearly 10,000 different platforms, there is a lot to track! To help, let's break down these products and solutions into four categories (Figure 2.3.2.1).

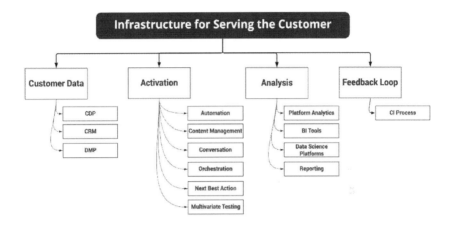

Figure 2.3.2.1, Infrastructure for Serving the Customer

Doing personalization well requires several components. An important one is the process and technology infrastructure needed to enable and improve personalization across a business. Let's explore this in more detail.

The infrastructure needs of personalization can be separated into four categories:
- Customer data
- Activation
- Analysis
- Feedback loop

Customer Data

Since we explored some of these terms in detail in the section on understanding the customer, I will briefly define each of these here:

- Customer data platforms (CDPs) provide a unified view of an individual consumer and often allow intelligent audience segmentation driven by manual and automated insights.
- Customer relationship management (CRM) systems capture sales, customer support, and marketing data that is often manually inputted or gathered from specific channels.
- Data management platforms (DMPs) collect data primarily related to advertising from third-party sources.
- Consent management platforms (CMPs) manage data privacy, opt-ins, and other risk-related data across an enterprise.

There may be other customer data or databases utilized by off-the-shelf products or custom-built customer databases that exist for one purpose or another.

This category is also affected by data privacy concerns and the necessary investments needed to meet standards and expectations. Because of this, marketers' technology investments are increasing in several key areas. Salesforce surveyed over 2,500 marketers worldwide and found that the top three categories where investments increased due to data privacy changes were marketing analytics and measurement technology (52%), CDP technology (50%), and real-time interaction and personalization technology (45%).[122]

One interesting takeaway here is that the two categories that have a direct relationship with data privacy—consent management technology and identity enrichment and resolution technology—were numbers four and five on that same list.

So, even regarding data privacy, platforms and technology related to personalized customer experiences are still top of mind.

Activation

The next category is the platforms that will enable personalization by coordinating and serving tailored messaging, offers, and actions to audience segments and individuals.

The activation category includes the following:
- Content management, which provides a repository of content variations used for personalization
- Customer journey orchestration, which can both dictate a customer flow as well as adjust to the journeys customers take most often
- Next best action, which can adjust to and predict the most likely behavior that will result in a conversion
- Conversation, which includes chatbots, conversational video, AI, and live chat
- Multivariate testing tools, which can automate testing according to personalized segments or individual user characteristics
  - Channel end points, which include anything serving content and experiences to consumers (e.g., websites, email service providers, mobile apps, live chat, and social ads)

Serving your customers with content and experiences personalized on a multichannel or omnichannel level is no easy feat. It requires a combination of people, processes, and platforms working in conjunction to be successful. These items also need to support the strategy, creation, delivery, and measurement of the content to provide the greatest value.

Providing personalized experience requires managing the content that reaches your audiences across those channels and ensuring you have the necessary workflows and tools to deliver the right message at the right time to the right customer.

Rather than relying on disconnected systems to store and manage content that should provide a consistent experience, it is a good idea to consider centralized content management. Although storing every piece of content in a single content management system (CMS) may not be feasible, technologies like headless CMSs make this more and more of a reality. A headless CMS separates the content itself from the formatting so that content can easily be stored regardless of the end point it will be displayed on.

This means that anything from web or mobile app content, push notifications, email content, text or SMS messages, and more can be stored in a single CMS.

Now, let's explore three key benefits of centralizing content management.

Workflow Efficiencies

Providing personalized content and experiences to your customers has the potential to produce great results, such as increasing key metrics like revenue per session and CLV. However, you will quickly realize that with greater personalization comes a need to create a greater volume and variation of content for distribution across multiple channels.

Creating multiple variations per audience per channel can add up quickly but providing a centralized content management system where assets are copied, repurposed, and reused can make this easier. This ease of creating content translates into increased productivity and allows your teams to spend more time on the strategy of content creation and less time on administrative tasks.

Centralized content management enables teams to focus on the best results rather than on moving content between systems and getting approvals—in addition to providing other efficiency gains.

Unified Taxonomy

The second benefit of centralized content management is that it encourages, or may force, a unified categorization or taxonomy of content within the system. This means that your content can more easily be tagged and grouped according to your personalization needs.

From my experience, a unified taxonomy will provide countless benefits as you integrate systems. Having your content, or at least most of it, in a centralized system makes this easier.

Setup for Ongoing Success

Although you can start building your House of the Customer brick by brick, it helps to use practices and platforms that will scale with you in the future. No one has a crystal ball, but storing your content in a centralized place helps you to be as future-forward as possible. It also means adjusting your categorization, taxonomy, or other modifications is easier since your content is all in one place.

New integration points for changes in platforms or even new platforms altogether also become easier to accommodate. Then, as your program matures to incorporate more audience segments, channels, localization, and so on, you are set up for greater success.

Analysis

This category includes platforms and tools that allow organizations to better understand the effectiveness of their personalization programs:

- CDPs with features that include at least some reporting and analysis (though most CDPs are not strongest in this area)
- DSPs that allow more robust number crunching
- Platform analytics that read data directly from the platforms
- Attribution platforms that specialize in stitching information together across channels and can assist when determining lift from personalization
- Other reporting tools that compile data from a variety of sources compiled together or look at large sets of data

Although approaches can vary widely, it's critical to have a holistic method of measuring and analyzing the effectiveness of your multichannel personalization efforts. Without this, you're simply guessing what works and what doesn't.

Feedback Loop

The final category refers to a needed process as much as a part of a technical infrastructure.

A feedback loop requires the findings uncovered through analysis, but it incorporates them into improvements in several areas:

- Audience segmentation
- Content
- Customer journey management
- Conversational AI

- Testing and hypotheses
- Attribution and measurement
- Internal processes

We will explore this concept of a feedback loop and continuous improvement more later in this book. For now, just remember that learning, adapting, and improving are key to both growing more efficiently as an organization and continually serving customers more effectively.

2.3.3 Mindset for Successful Personalized Experiences

If delivering a robust personalized, omnichannel customer experience was easy, all your peers would be doing it already. Instead, many enterprises and smaller organizations are delivering multichannel experiences at best, with many still spearheading siloed approaches.

That said, delivering customers a multi- or omnichannel experience is not science fiction. It can be done incrementally over time, ultimately delivering that seamless experience that many consumers are already expecting.

In this chapter, we'll talk about how to deliver an omnichannel customer experience, even if you're still on the path to achieving it. Let's get started!

Stay Customer Centric, Not Platform Focused

Although your priority may be a customer-facing effort, it's easy to get drawn into the details of platform functionality, API integration requirements, and data compatibility issues. These items can be so distracting that discussions around them may derail an initiative from its original goal of enhancing the customer journey.

Platforms and integrations may change over time. Although these are critical components, remember the reason you're doing it in the first place: to make a great, seamless customer experience. Therefore, you should ensure that your primary requirements are what the *customer* needs to see, do, and receive in exchange for their interactions. Important as they are, internal operational requirements and legacy system requirements need to be treated as secondary priorities.

Doing this will help you avoid getting too far into a project or multi-phase initiative and realize that you've lost sight of the customer.

Keep the Journey in Mind

Are your customers having an uneven experience as they progress through the buyer's journey? If you have integrated some steps to provide a multichannel experience, your customers are likely to notice the difference when they encounter a channel that's still siloed. There can be many reasons for this.

Although you may start your omnichannel work at a single stage of the journey through proof of concept or a pilot project, make sure you're thinking of the entire journey. Getting things perfect at one step can even cause confusion if they feel as though one hand isn't talking to the other somewhere else down the line.

Don't confuse this for a recommendation to try to tackle everything at once. Agile, iterative improvements and additions can build amazing results in the long run. Instead, make sure that you are at least thinking about the big picture as you work on pieces of the larger customer journey one (or a few) at a time.

Experimentation Is Key

Keep experimenting and optimizing! What works well today might not work well tomorrow, even with the same audience on the same channel.

With the world (and our customers) in constant flux, it's important to maintain a mindset of testing and experimentation.

In fact, Braze's "Customer Engagement Review" found that brands considered leaders in customer engagement are 2.3 times more likely to actively experiment with customer journeys across channels.[123]

Build for the Future

One of the reasons I am so in favor of agile methods is that they allow organizations and individuals to adjust their approaches without deviating from an overall strategy and set of goals.

Keep in mind that you don't know what you don't know. In other words, stay agnostic in your approach to integrating systems and building components within your existing framework. When utilizing larger systems, such as marketing platforms or digital experience hubs, make sure they have the maturity and product roadmaps to support future needs, including the ability to integrate external systems you may need down the road.

Building for the future means acknowledging that new, unanticipated needs will arise over time. This may involve people, processes, or technology—likely all three—that are not on your current slate of objectives. Think modularly as you build and integrate systems, and think flexibly when creating processes. Your future internal teams and your customers will thank you!

Doing an omnichannel customer experience well requires balancing several priorities with the people, processes, and platforms that support them, all while always keeping a focus on the customer. Whether you are just starting down the path to personalized multichannel customer experience or your organization is close to reaching an omnichannel reality, keep these ideas in mind for continued success.

2.4 Pillar 4: Listening to the Customer

One of the most sincere forms of respect is actually listening to what another has to say.
—Bryant H. McGill

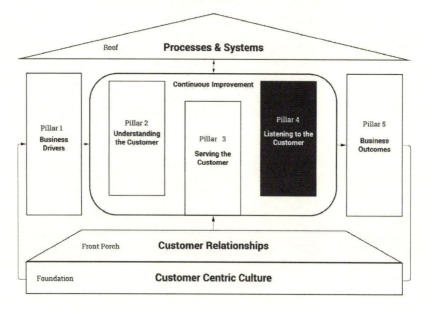

Figure 2.4.1, Pillar 4: Listening to the Customer

In 60 AD, well before the age of customer experience, the Greek philosopher Epictetus said, "We have two ears and one mouth so that we can listen twice as much as we speak."[124] Many marketers and communications would do well to heed those words of wisdom!

The first and obvious reason is that your customers have valuable information and insights that can help you improve your business. The second might be less direct but is no less important. Although no leader will argue that customers aren't important to their organization, prioritization of customer satisfaction in terms of time and resources varies widely.

For instance, in Salesforce's "Marketing Intelligence Report," 46% of the over 2,500 marketers surveyed stated that customer satisfaction was a top metric defining their success, with only 35% of them saying they are completely successful at evaluating that success.[125]

This is where listening to the customer, our fourth pillar of the House of the Customer, comes into play.

North Star State

The ideal state of our fourth pillar, Listening to the Customer, builds on everything we've discussed so far. When we can provide a personalized, omnichannel customer experience, it is critical that we are also able to measure and understand the components of that customer journey. This means measuring at both an individual level as well as a higher level that allows you to see how those pieces work together. This is where the ability to engage in multi-touch attribution becomes increasingly important, and it's why I devote an entire chapter to it.

The North Star state of listening to the customer is when we can see which channels and communication methods are performing strongly and what we can do to enable the interplay of different channels and experiences to improve customer lifetime value.

When this pillar is done well, it leads perfectly to the fifth and final pillar: Business Outcomes.

What We Will Cover

In this section of the book, we are going to look at the different dimensions and categories that are important to include as we measure the customer experience. We will also look at attribution, particularly multi-touch attribution (MTA), as a means of understanding the different channels within a multichannel or omnichannel experience.

Let's get started!

2.4.1 Measurement, Analysis, and Reporting

John Wanamaker, considered by many to be a pioneer in marketing, has contributed to the field one of the most-quoted lines about advertising: "Half the money I spend on advertising is wasted; the trouble is I don't know which half."

John Wanamaker isn't alone. In eMarketer's recent report, only half of US advertisers were satisfied with their marketing campaign measurement, with paid search and paid social providing the most satisfaction at 50%, and digital video providing the least at 38%.[126]

After all, what good is it to spend the considerable effort it takes to build your House of the Customer, only to fail to understand how effective your personalized experiences are with your customers? Let's explore this now.

How Do You Measure Personalized Experiences?

Let's explore how personalization is measured by looking at three categories of measurement, and their components (Figure 2.4.1.1).

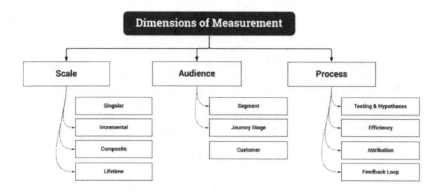

Figure 2.4.1.1, Dimensions of Measurement

Scale

Scale refers to how comprehensive the measurements are across channels and audiences. Let's explore each of the two subcategories now.

Singular Measurements

As the name suggests, these measurements are single metrics, such as the number of clicks on an advertisement or a button on a website, the number of sales to a single customer, or a myriad of other points of data you have access to. Suffice it to say, you are probably flooded with singular metrics, and that can make it difficult to know what to do with them. As we'll see, these singular metrics become more valuable as they are used to build complex measurements.

That said, looking at specific measures can help diagnose opportunities as well as challenges that broader metrics may gloss over.

Incremental Measurements

These refer to singular measurements that provide a lift versus ones without personalization. In other words, it's the result of personalizing content by audience segment (or individual) versus showing every customer the exact same content.

Some of the measurements include measuring the incremental improvements or lift by providing:
- A personalized experience versus no personalization
- Cross-channel personalization versus personalization on a single channel (or none)
- Single-channel performance utilizing personalization versus not using personalization on that channel

Additionally, these can be expressed as changes in a metric over points of time. Although the nomenclature can be confusing, I often refer to these incremental measurements as *performance* measurements because they more easily demonstrate positive or negative changes over time and can be more prescriptive than a single metric.

Composite Measurements

As the name suggests, these measurements look at multiple channels and points in time. This category also includes some of the tried-and-true qualitative measures that many CX and marketing professionals rely on.

For instance, the formula for customer retention rate, while simple, requires more than a single number, and utilizes the component of a time range:

Retention Rate (%) = (Number of Customers at End of Period − Number of Customers Acquired During Period) / Total Number of Customers at Start of Period

As there are several composite measures listed below (and more that aren't included), I'm not going to provide a formula for all of them. However, I've categorized the measurements for ease of reading:

Acquisition

- Customer acquisition cost
- Cost per acquisition
- Return on ad spend

Revenue/Orders

- Revenue per customer
- Revenue per session
- Average order value

Conversion/Retention

- Conversion rate
- Customer churn rate
- Customer retention rate
- Upsell and cross-sell Rate

Satisfaction

- Net promoter score (NPS)
- Customer satisfaction (CSAT)
- Customer effort score (CES)
- Time to resolution

Journey

- Journey stage performance
- Journey performance (as a whole)
- Journey performance per customer

Another category of composite measurements is self-created metrics, which compile several data points and statistics together to show a snapshot of the health of customer experience, satisfaction, or engagement. These are often called engagement scores and take several internal metrics to create.

These can often be helpful as a relative measure over time, but I advise being cautious of how much you rely on them. Although understanding the trajectory of a single score can tell you something about the overall health of your efforts, it can often be difficult to diagnose what went right (or wrong). Just as bad, these run the risk of being vanity metrics that are slapped onto reports without anyone truly understanding the impact of an increase or decrease.

Lifetime

Tracking the scale of customer lifetime uses metrics such as customer lifetime value (CLV), cost per acquisition (CPA), and other metrics that not only require calculation across multiple channels and sources, but their timing also spans the entire lifecycle of the buyer's journey.

It should be noted that these metrics present big challenges to organizations. A recent survey from SharpSpring and Ascend2 in April 2022 of 329 sales and marketing professionals reported that only 20% of organizations currently have the ability to track the customer lifecycle end-to-end.[127] In that same survey, about half (53%) said they could mostly track the customer lifecycle. Unfortunately, "mostly" isn't enough to cut it in most cases. What's worse, over one quarter of respondents (26%) said they were either "not really" or "not at all" able to track customer lifecycle.

We're going to talk more about these later.

Audience

Audience measures what you might expect—customers—in a few different ways. Although this may sound straightforward enough, marketers continue to be challenged by collecting and maintaining accurate data about their customers and audience. In fact, Nielsen's

2022 "Era of Alignment" report shows that only 26% of global marketers are fully confident about their audience data.[128]

Better processes, systems, and methods of categorizing audience data can help improve this. Let's look at the ways I categorize audience data.

Audience Segments

Audience segments are groupings of customers by demographics, interest areas, ownership of a particular product or subscription, or other customer dimensions. Audience segments may share some similar characteristics from one organization to another, but each brand and its customers will likely have different attribute combinations.

Measuring the Segments

Your personalization efforts should include methods to measure the performance of your audience segments as well as ways to refine them. For instance, your segmentation may be too broad and include audience members that are less likely to convert.

Measuring Content against Segments

In addition to measuring your segments and how they perform against the content and experience you provide, you can also measure how your personalized content performs with different audience segments. This will show areas where your personalized content and experience need to be strengthened by looking at it from several unique audience perspectives.

Personas

You may also be familiar with the concept of personas, which are often used to visualize and build user stories when creating new products and experiences. Although personas are not a substitute for audience segments, they can be helpful when hypothesizing which audience segments will be most valuable.

Measuring your audience segments will help you understand whether some of these hypotheses were right or not.

Journey and Journey Stage

The next category includes both measurement of the overall journey as well as individual journey stages. Although individual journey stages are more straightforward to measure because there is less data to crunch, it is important to measure the overall journey as well, particularly when customer lifetime value (CLV) is a key metric. If you find yourself challenged by reporting on the full journey, you are not alone. According to Nielsen's 2022 "Era of Alignment" report, only 54% of global marketers surveyed are confident in their ability to measure ROI within the full funnel or journey.[129]

In addition to measuring progress through the overall customer journey, there should also be measurements at individual journey stages to identify where a customer might buy multiple products, need customer or technical support, and have the opportunity to refer others, as illustrated in the figure below (Figure 2.4.1.2):

Customer Journey

Figure 2.4.1.2, Customer Journey

It is important to measure personalization through initial awareness of your brand, product, or service, all the way to purchase and activation. Utilizing journey orchestration and next-best-action tools can greatly enhance this, particularly when those tools have their own data-collection and measurement functionality. By feeding those metrics into the rest of your measurement data, you get a comprehensive look at audience segment by channel and journey stage.

Although your audience segments may include an attribute for each journey stage, you may want to consider making journey stage an independent attribute or variable instead of a defining characteristic of the audience segment. Doing so will allow you to measure different journey stages both inclusive and exclusive of a specific audience segment.

Individual Customer

Although working with larger groups can be easier, it is important to continuously measure individuals throughout the process for many reasons.

Obviously, you need to measure individual customers because you need that data to enable customer-support opportunities, individualized communications, and other activities.

Additionally, as you move toward a one-to-one personalization approach, you will need to increasingly understand how and why individuals perform certain actions. It's also helpful in determining why they respond better to one type of content over another and provides a mechanism to personalize content on a more individualized basis.

Process

The last category, Process, measures the systems and methods used to perform personalization, how those systems perform, and how they are improved. Some of these enable you to measure the process of personalization itself, providing a meta view to assess your systems as a whole.

Hypothesis and Testing

First, there is the process of testing itself. This should follow the scientific method, which includes anywhere from five to seven steps. I like to use the simpler five-step process as follows:

1. Define a question or hypothesis.
2. Make a prediction to test the hypothesis.
3. Perform the test by gathering relevant data.
4. Analyze the data.
5. Draw a conclusion.

Maintaining Efficiency

You could make the argument (and I would agree) that efficiency is always important. That said, in the case of personalization and achieving ROI, it is very easy for time, costs, and other resources to expand considerably if they remain unchecked.

Because of the need for increased content creation to account for the multiple variants required by personalization, the process needs to become more efficient.

There are several ways to do this. A few potential methods include
- Utilizing an agile, sprint-based approach (e.g., two weeks for each phase of the content creation process) and measuring their efficiency (e.g, Are deadlines getting missed or other projects slipping?)
- Finding methods to automate portions of the process, such as image creation or localization of content
- Utilizing AI tools to quickly identify relevant images in a large database (e.g., using image recognition to detect photos that feature a specific product, number of people, or type of location)
- Implementing a shared content management system where content can be stored and repurposed easily

As with everything, make sure your efforts to create more efficiency don't get in the way of the actual work that needs to be done! Start small if needed, but build a plan that ensures you grow efficiently as your personalization efforts scale.

Attribution

Put simply, this means that sources, channels, and methods get the credit (or blame!) for an interaction. As you can imagine, personalized, omnichannel customer experiences have several touch points; thus, attribution is extremely important but not without challenges.

Why is this so important? Because marketing and advertising dollars and resources are at stake and often going toward efforts that are either ineffective or hard to quantify in terms of effectiveness. Recent research from sales and marketing professionals by SharpSpring and Ascend2 revealed that only 21% of those surveyed felt confident in their ability to prove ROI and the effectiveness of individual campaigns.[130] Attribution provides the answer to whether or not efforts are working.

Let's explore some of the available methods of attribution.

First-Touch or Last-Touch

First-touch or last-touch assumes that the placement of a touch point in the customer journey—first or last—makes it more important when attributing to a conversion. These stand in starkest contrast to multitouch attribution, which we'll get to in a minute.

There are obvious shortcomings with this method, particularly in a world where 80% of the top one hundred retailers in the world offer some form of channel-switching option for their customers.[131]

Still, many organizations use this method based on its ease of use to calculate the effectiveness of touch points in the customer journey.

Incrementality

If you want to go beyond first-touch or last-touch attribution but aren't quite able to do multitouch attribution, incrementality testing might be a viable option. In this approach, instead of trying to measure every source to calculate attribution, you perform a series of multivariate tests. In each test, you add and remove sources and channels from the test to determine the ones that are most effective.

You could almost call this a form of testing rather than attribution. That said, success with incremental testing allows you to model different forms of attribution that can helpful you analyze the results of your personalized customer experiences.

Multi-Touch Attribution

To use holistic measurements, you will need to utilize better attribution methods, including multi-touch attribution (MTA). As you might remember, this is also one of our North Star goals for the House of the Customer.

Although challenges remain, MTA is increasingly used by marketers everywhere. According to the most recent MMA Global Marketing Attribution Think Tank (MATT) report, while only 27% of marketers are currently fully deploying MTA, there has been a nearly 33% increase in the adoption of MTA over the last year (2021 to 2022).[132]

We'll explore this topic more in the next chapter, but if you're going to personalize across channels, you need to understand which pieces of your personalization are working best.

Feedback Loops

Of course, what good is all this audience, content, and process measurement if we don't have a method to leverage those findings to incrementally improve over time?

Creating a feedback loop will allow you to take all your personalization ROI measurements and channel them into improving how things are done in the future. Ideally this feedback loop has both human and automated components. This will allow teams to communicate insights and ideas that may be more subjective in nature.

Then, the other more automated measurements can provide recommendations in a more objective manner.

Some of the items you should create feedback loops around include the following:

- The accuracy and performance of audience segmentation
- The impact of content variations, including messaging, images, and calls to action
- Customer journey performance and journey definitions
- The quality of testing and hypotheses
- Attribution measurement quality
- Internal process performance from objective and subjective perspectives

Conclusion

In such a competitive environment, brands can't afford to simply do personalization. Instead, they need clear plans to measure and improve their efforts over time. Remember, customer experience is a competitive advantage for brands that get it right.

This competitive advantage will only last if you perpetuate your efforts. Measuring the performance of your personalization in the ways described above can help you keep up and pull ahead.

In the next chapter, we're going to take a deeper dive into multi-touch attribution since it will play such an important role in your personalized experiences and in measuring the outcomes of your House of the Customer.

2.4.2 Preparing for Multi-Touch Attribution

We've discussed multi-touch attribution (MTA) a few times already, so in this chapter, we're going to explore ways to successfully prepare for and implement MTA.

A customer goes through an average of six touch points before converting.[133] This is important because every touch point customers have with your brand influences their decision to convert. MTA helps you understand each touch point's role in converting customers and generating revenue.

When done effectively, MTA accounts for every touch point on the buyer's journey and designates credit to each channel based on its effectiveness in driving conversion. With MTA, you can now allocate your marketing spend appropriately. Preparing for MTA success also involves answering a number of questions, which we will explore now.

Define Your Goals

Any marketing attribution effort begins with clearly defined goals. This applies to MTA as well. As you set out, you must know what you're aiming to achieve by the end. Defining goals will help you select the most suitable model for your business based on the customer journey, which can be complex.

When you clearly set goals from the start, you can do the following.

Understand Channel Performance

Through MTA, you learn which channels and marketing tactics drive performance and generate a high ROI. This enables you to optimize within these channels while helping with planning and forecasting.

Understand Campaign Performance

Initially, advertising attribution posed a significant challenge for marketers. Luckily, MTA is the answer. After you've set your goals, you know what level of success you need from each marketing campaign. You should be prepared to act on attribution findings for long-term planning and real-time campaign adjustments.

Understand Your Customers

Today's consumer has become adept at avoiding marketing messages. As such, you should seek to understand your audience to better curate messages and campaigns that resonate with them. A survey found that 76% of customers expect companies to understand their needs.[134] MTA offers granular data that enables you to identify audiences across all channels and determine the specific marketing desires of those users.

Once you understand the audience and their needs based on the data collected, you can apply those insights to correct mistakes and create a more customized experience. Improving your consumer experience should always be one of the top goals for your marketing efforts. According to research by Deloitte, customer-centric companies are 60% more profitable than those that aren't.[135]

Define Your Measurements

Before you adopt an MTA model, you must determine the KPIs that align with your marketing goals. You'll then use those KPIs to assess the success of your MTA efforts. Are your efforts driving the desired actions and outcomes? Are the goals you set being achieved?

KPIs allow you to see how you're performing, where you're exceeding expectations, and where you need to make improvements. Most marketers who implement MTA are looking to improve their ROI and user experience, so the metrics that measure the success or failure of MTA must reflect these goals and what they mean for the specific organization.

Understand the Journey

Very few customers will make a purchase on their first visit to your site. In most cases, they hop from one device or channel to another, also known as channel switching. This switching can occur after seeing ads, getting referrals from friends, and reading blogs. For this reason, MTA is critical to spotting effective user-acquisition channels.

MTA is most successful when you can incorporate all the meaningful customer touch points into your measurements. It takes account of the cost of each touch point and the importance it's given as part of the customer journey. MTA then compares that relationship to the value it contributes to conversion. With visibility of all touch points along the consumer's journey, your teams can make informed decisions for future campaigns.

Implementing MTA involves getting all the touch points across the devices, channels, and platforms to communicate with each other. This enables your teams to develop holistic marketing campaigns that reflect the buyer's journey.

Although easier said than done, it is increasingly important to understand the impact of individual steps along the customer journey. This allows you to continue delivering optimal personalized customer experiences and to understand its impact on your business.

2.5 Pillar 5: Business Outcomes

If you accept the expectations of others, especially negative ones, then you never will change the outcome.
—Michael Jordan

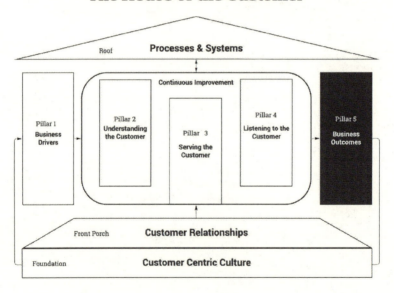

Figure 2.5.1, Pillar 5: Business Outcomes

We've spent a lot of time talking about the benefits of building a House of the Customer from the customer perspective, but now it's time to focus on ROI and other benefits to the organization.

These impacts can be significant. In the "2022 Twilio State of Customer Engagement Report," companies worldwide attributed 70% of their 2021 revenue increases to investments in digital customer engagement, with respondents from the United States driving that number all the way up to 79%.[136] This makes sense, considering the COVID-19 pandemic was still in full force at this point, but it underscores the importance of investing in building your own House of the Customer.

The fifth and final pillar of our House of the Customer is called Business Outcomes, and it is the culmination of everything we've built so far but looked at from the business's perspective. We still have two more parts of our house to explore, but this section focuses on the bottom line, LTV of customers, and ROI of transformation initiatives. With this information, your organization can deliver the omnichannel personalized experiences we've discussed.

North Star State

To examine our ideal state of the Business Outcomes pillar, we should look at it through a few lenses.

First, the business should have a thorough *understanding* of the business outcomes. Although that may sound obvious or elementary, you would be surprised by how many organizations struggle to understand (for example) the LTV of their customers. So, one piece of the North Star state is that the business can use what it's learned by understanding, reaching, and serving to understand the impacts on the business.

Second, the business should have *context* for its outcomes. Where are your strengths and weaknesses as an organization? Where are your competitors in relation to where you are now and where you're headed? Where is your industry headed? Where are your customers headed?

Finally, the business should understand its *trajectory*. Where are you now compared to where you were? Where are you headed and on how steep (or shallow) a curve?

When an organization can embrace these three lenses, the Business Outcomes pillar of the House of the Customer can be successful.

What We Will Cover

In this section on Business Outcomes, we're going to discuss the key performance indicators (KPIs) that can be used to measure the success of our House of the Customer.

I will also be introducing a maturity model that utilizes the elements of our House to identify areas of growth and challenge. This will help with both the context and trajectory aspects of our North Star state.

With that said, we're ready to move on!

2.5.1 KPIs for the House of the Customer

In the last section, we looked at several aspects of listening to our customers and ensuring we put them at the center of the house, so to speak. As we explore the fifth pillar of our house, we're going to look at how to measure success in relation to business growth. At the end of the day, we need our customer-centric approach to translate into tangible business outcomes.

What Is at Stake?

From a results perspective, customers speak with their wallets. The recent Zendesk report provides several insights here, including the following statistics pulled from respondents in North America:

- 91% of consumers will spend more with companies that offer their preferred method of communication with customer service.
- 88% of consumers will spend more with companies that ensure they won't need to repeat information.
- 86% of consumers will spend more with companies that personalize the customer service they offer.[137]

What does this mean for your business? Customers who buy more will buy more often and tell their friends, which drives the type of business outcomes we need. To clarify, while there are many outcomes

possible for a business, I'm primarily talking about the following types of measures:
1. Revenue and profit (more accurately, gross and net profit margin)
2. Sales revenue, sales growth, and monthly recurring revenue
3. Sustainability of the business

What's more, the research backs this up. According to research by Medallia Institute comparing CX leaders and "laggards," CX leaders are twenty-six times more likely to experience revenue growth of 20% or more over the past fiscal year. Additionally, CX leaders are 2.8 times more likely than laggards to meet financial targets and be viewed as a great place to work.[138]

It doesn't take a chief financial officer to know that any of these alone is not enough, but those are the types of measurements we need to create a direct line between customer experience and the bottom line.

Business Outcome KPIs Versus Customer KPIs and Metrics

In discussing the fourth pillar of our House, we looked at several ways to listen to customers, including specific metrics, methods, and scales of measurement. Those are critical to gaining a true view of your customers, their experiences, and their overall journey.

When we shift to look at things from a business outcome perspective, we want to tie those customer-centric and journey-centric analytics to the bottom line. To do this, we must introduce KPIs that bridge the gap between customer experience and business outcomes.

We also want to make sure that we follow best practices when determining what makes a good KPI. For this, we look to Investopedia, which argues a strong KPI has these four attributes:

- Provides objective and clear information on progress toward an end goal
- Tracks and measures factors such as efficiency, quality, timeliness, and performance
- Provides a way to measure performance over time
- Helps leadership make more informed decisions[139]

Let's explore the four customer KPIs I recommend as part of the business outcomes metrics of your House of the Customer.

Customer Acquisition Cost (CAC)

As much as we want to create engaged and loyal customers, we still need to generate new ones. As for this KPI, the name pretty much says it all. Here's a quick formula to help calculate it:

Customer Acquisition Cost (CAC) = Sales and Marketing Costs / Number of New Customers

Let's plug in a few numbers to show how this works:
- Sales and marketing costs = $1 million
- New customers = 25,000

Therefore, CAC = $40, or $1 million divided by 25,000.

Retention Rate

Retention Rate (%) = (Number of Customers at End of Period − Number of Customers Acquired During Period) / Total Number of Customers at Start of Period

Let's plug in some real numbers here as well:
- Number of customer at the start of the period: 1,000

- Number of customers acquired during the period: 250
- Number of customers at end of period: 1,100

Retention Rate = (1,110 − 250) / 1,000, or 85%.

Although we covered this in the "Listening to the Customer" section, I wanted to impress it's importance. For instance, an increase of even 5% in customer retention rate can produce 25% or more increase in profits, according to research by Bain & Company.[140] That's why I treat it as a primary KPI.

Net Promoter Score (NPS) or Customer Satisfaction (CSAT)

Those who follow my blog and writing know that I am less than kind to these measurements at times, but I must admit that they can be a valuable snapshot of the customer relationship at points in time. However, for them to be successful, they must be tied to financial outcomes and not used as a sole metric of success or failure.

I also acknowledge that many organizations have been using one or both of these for many years, and legacy data can be extremely valuable.

Customer Lifetime Value (CLV)

If you aren't familiar with how to calculate customer lifetime value (CLV), here's a simple version provided by OmniConvert from their blog:

Customer Lifetime Value [CLV] =
(Purchase Frequency [PF] × Average Order Value [AOV] × Gross Margin [GM] × Customer Lifespan [CL])
/ Number of New Customers[141]

Let's define the terms to make sure it's all clear:

- ***Purchase Frequency (PF):*** *This is how often the average customer makes a purchase from you. Choose a measurement for frequency that makes sense for your business. For instance, a car manufacturer and a quick service restaurant are going to have different time frequencies that make sense. The former might be in years and the latter in weeks.*
- ***Average Order Value (AOV):*** *This is the average amount a customer spends with your brand.*
- ***Gross Margin (GM):*** *This helps you calculate the amount of profit you make on each order, and gets to a much more accurate number than simply using the Average Order Value (AOV) as your measurement of how much you make from the average customer.*
- ***Customer Lifespan (CL):*** *Again, make sure to make this in the same unit of measurement of your purchase frequency (weeks, months, years).*
- ***Number of New Customers:*** *This is the number of new customers you gain within the same unit of frequency chosen for purchase frequency and customer lifespan.*

Note that LTV is sometimes used as well. LTV is the lifetime spend of customers in the aggregate. Although LTV has its uses, it is often more valuable to look at lifetime value on the customer level.

Investing in a first- and zero-party data approach can also pay off when showing CLV. Forrester's 2022 report based on 200 North American and EMEA marketing decision-makers shows that 76% consider the most transformational benefit of investing in data strategies is increased CLV (followed closely by 75% stating improved customer profiling due to enriched data [75%] and an improved ability to target customers [74%]).[142]

Related to CLV, a 2022 report by customer engagement platform Braze showed that customer engagement leaders have an 89% longer average customer lifetime.[143] Although this doesn't necessarily add up to more dollars over that period, increasing customer lifetime increases the opportunity to create more value.

Employee Engagement Score or Retention Rate

Let's not forget the people doing the work! I strongly believe that an employee metric should be included in your KPIs. However, this depends on your organization and the metrics you have previously used to measure employee engagement, satisfaction, and retention.

I wrote an entire book, *The Center of Experience*, about the relationship between customer and employee experience. I believe strongly that people-based metrics should be in your KPIs for your House of the Customer.

Putting Them Together

When we combine these metrics, they tell a story:
1. How easily are we getting new customers? (CAC)
2. Are we engaging and retaining them? (Customer Retention)
3. How satisfied are our customers and likely to share with others? (NPS or CSAT)
4. What value can we assign to a loyal, satisfied customer? (CLV)

5. How sustainable are our teams that create CX and are responsible for knowledge transfer and product innovation? (Employee Engagement or Retention)

We'll explore the employee component of this more in the next section as well. It is important to align all these human metrics with financial metrics. The more correlation you can show between the two, the better.

Reporting on Trajectory

In addition to reporting on the KPIs themselves, it is important to look at the trajectory between points in time. I often refer to this as measuring performance, as it shows percentage increases or decreases while also giving more context and perspective.

That said, seasonality and other factors must be considered when looking at trajectory. This may factor into choosing between month-over-month, quarter-over-quarter, or year-over-year metrics.

2.5.2 Organizational Maturity

Although it's important to measure the individual business outcomes and KPIs we've already discussed, how do you measure your progress in building your House of the Customer?

Improving Measurement Sophistication Over Time

Since we're talking about the ROI of personalized customer experiences, it's important to understand that your House of the Customer will be a work in progress for a while.

First and foremost, as we talked about in the last chapter, make sure that you have overall KPIs defined for your House of the Customer. Even if your goal is to increase the CLV, you may want to start with a more immediate focus and, for example, increase the revenue per session of customers that see personalized content.

Then, you can build your measurement sophistication as you add channels and thus increase the integrations needed for MTA.

To start, create a roadmap for your data, integrations, attributions, and measurements of success. You may not be able to start with your ideal scenario, but you can have a plan to get there and use the steps along your roadmap to continually justify greater investments in personalization.

The House of the Customer Maturity Model

Improvement of individual metrics can demonstrate progress, but it's more helpful to show broader, sustained growth. This is particularly true when substantial investments of time and resources are needed. For this reason, tracking success against a maturity model can be helpful.

This also highlights the failures of much of the thinking and writing about maturity models in general. Most seem to be a relatively static measurement of where a company is rather than a gauge of the company in continual motion.

For this reason, an organization should regularly measure itself against the maturity model I propose. And because it is directly aligned with the components of the House of the Customer, you can easily diagnose where you stand in each of the important components.

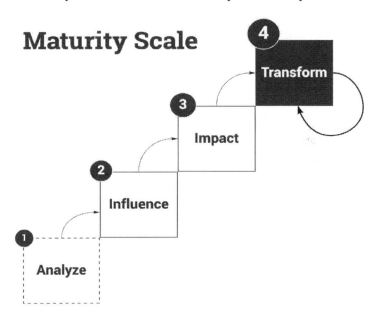

Figure 2.5.2.1, Organizational Maturity Scale

The House of the Customer maturity model has four stages (Figure 2.5.2.1), each named for the type of strategic thinking, prioritization, and investment needed to build a House of the Customer and the relationship it has with the organization. It's similar to other maturity models in that the lowest number represents the least mature organization.

Let's briefly review each of the stages.

Analyze

In this stage, there is no common understanding within an organization that one-to-one omnichannel personalized experiences will transform the business and its customer relationships. There may be supporters in the organization, but there will still be skeptics who need proof of the ROI. Sound familiar? If that's the case, your organization is in the Analyze phase, where there is research and possibly a pilot project or two under development.

Influence

In the second stage, a few successful pilot projects and some outspoken advocates have gotten the North Star goals to be taken seriously within the organization. At this point, the momentum is starting to influence budgetary and resource allocations that could pave the way for better personalized experiences. Still, the North Star goals are years away from being realized in full.

Impact

When we reach the Impact stage, the pilot projects have given way to full-fledged multiyear initiatives, and leadership is aware of the impact reaching North Star goals can have on the organization. Although there is still work to be done, investments of time, resources, and dollars already made are having an impact on customer growth and retention as well as the bottom line.

Transform

In the Transform stage, at least some of our North Star goals are being accomplished, and all or most of the others are nearly reached. Organizations in the Transform stage have achieved sustainable growth driven by great multi- or omnichannel experiences, which factors into their strategic decision-making. They are also continually striving to improve and stay ahead of the competition.

The Dimensions of Maturity

In addition to stages, we measure maturity according to seven dimensions that map to the House of the Customer. Although we've already explored each of these in terms of implementing a House of the Customer, let's explore each as they pertain to the maturity model. Each dimension has three components, and when the maturity assessment is done, participants rate each of the three subdimensions related to the main seven.

Business Drivers

This domain relates to *strategy* and has the following subdimensions:
- Clarity of vision
- Communication of vision
- Measurable goals definition

Understanding the Customer

This domain relates to *customer data* and has the following subdimensions:

- Completeness of data
- Quality of data
- Data infrastructure

Serving the Customer

This domain relates to *platforms and personalized experiences* and has the following subdimensions:

- Quality of the omnichannel experience
- Experience infrastructure
- Journey orchestration across channels

Listening to the Customer

This domain relates to *measurement and feedback loops* and has the following subdimensions:

- Attribution across channels
- Prioritization of efforts based on measurement
- Measurement infrastructure

Business Outcomes

This domain relates to *ROI-related results* and has the following subdimensions:

- Execution of vision
- Achievement of measurable goals
- Continuous improvement

Customer Centric Culture

This domain relates to an *organizational culture that supports great experience* and has the following subdimensions:

- Strong culture definition

- Culture alignment
- Trajectory of cultural alignment

Customer Relationships

This domain relates to a company's relationship with customers and has the following subdimensions:

- Customer acquisition
- Customer satisfaction
- Customer retention

As you can see, this multidimensional look at how your organization is performing can help you find direct alignment with the categories that make up our House of the Customer.

How Your Organization Stacks Up

In my research for this book, I compared the dimensions of the maturity model to multiple sources that surveyed tens of thousands of business leaders and managers across dimensions. All sources were written within two years of this book's publication to make the data as relevant as possible.

First, let's look at overall maturity (Figure 2.5.2.2):

Overall Personalized Experience Maturity

An analysis of companies across 7 scales using the House of the Customer model

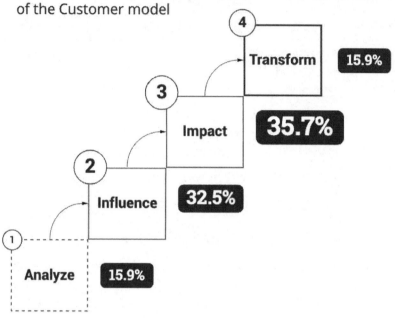

Figure 2.5.2.2, Overall Personalized Experience Maturity

Now let's look at maturity in each of the subcategories measured in the maturity scale:

HOUSE OF THE CUSTOMER

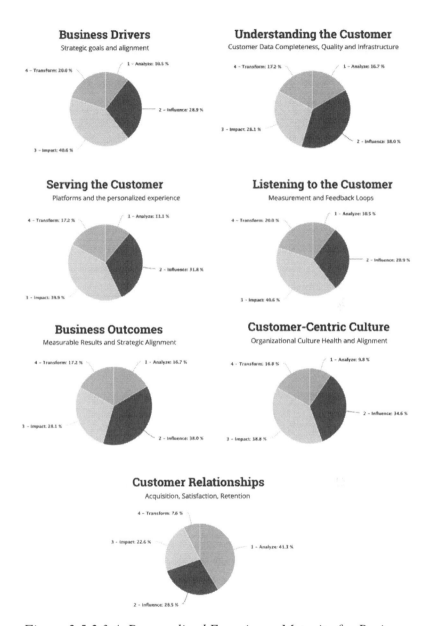

Figure 2.5.2.3,4, Personalized Experience Maturity for Business Drivers, Understanding the Customer, Serving the Customer, and Listening to the Customer, Business Outcomes, Customer-Centric Culture, and Customer Relationships

A few insights immediately jump out from Figures 2.5.2.3 and 2.5.2.4. First, companies tend toward the middle of the maturity scale, with a few exceptions. Generally, we have about as many leaders in level 4 of the scale as we do laggards in level 1. This is also reflected in the overall maturity scale.

To learn more about the process and sources I used to calculate average scores, refer to appendix I, where I list all sources and a little more information on the methodology itself.

Use It for Your Organization

There are many reasons to use a maturity model, but in my experience, one of the most important ones is that it serves as a barometer.

To make it easy to use the House of the Customer maturity model, I've included a spreadsheet version as part of the online materials that accompany this book. Just go to https://houseofthecustomer.com/ to download the materials.

Conclusion

Using a maturity scale like the one provided can help you set measurable targets and track your progress toward them. Such scales are also helpful in ensuring company-wide alignment and understanding of important areas for growth and improvement.

In the next section, I'm going to talk about the foundation of our House of the Customer: customer relationships.

2.6: The Front Porch: Customer Relationships

A British porch is a musty, forbidding non-room in which to fling a sodden umbrella or a muddy pair of boots; a guard against the elements and strangers. By contrast the good ol' American front porch seems to stand for positivity and openness; a platform from which to welcome or wave farewell; a place where things of significance could happen.
—Dan Stevens

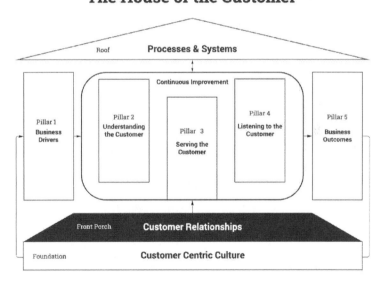

Figure 2.6.1, The Front Porch: Customer Relationships

Every company claims to "love" their customers and says the customer is "number one." However, the proof, as they say, is in the pudding. Companies that invest in great customer experiences and relationships will, time and time again, reap the benefits of those investments.

That said, even companies that *believe* they're doing well may not be having the effect they desire. For instance, according to a recent Coresight Research report, 71% of the brands and retailers surveyed claimed to be excelling in marketing personalization and digital experiences, yet only 34% of consumers felt the same way.[144]

Hence, our focus is on this seventh and final element of our House of the Customer: the front porch. Here we build and maintain customer relationships so that those customers buy, buy more, and tell others about the brand.

For this section, we're going to assume that good customer relationships are valuable to the business, and that the business understands the relationship between delivering great CX and the bottom line. If you are looking for more substantiation of this, I recommend referring to the wealth of good books, white papers, and blogs on the topic.

North Star State

In our ideal state for customer relationships, the following is true:
- Our cost of new customer acquisition is low because of positive word of mouth and a well-orchestrated buyer's journey.
- Our customer engagement and customer satisfaction are high because of the seamless experience we deliver.
- Our customer loyalty and customer retention are high because we listen to and respond to our customers' needs.

- Our current customers often refer new customers who grow into loyal customers themselves.

As you can see, the above criteria include the full customer life cycle. The measurements used to determine success may vary, but all directly relate to metrics and KPIs discussed earlier in this book.

What We Will Cover

We're going to define what makes a good customer relationship in the context of personalized experiences, then talk about the customer types that get incorporated into the House of the Customer model.

2.6.1 What Makes a Good Customer Relationship?

In this chapter, I'm going to discuss the key principles that comprise a good customer relationship. I am going to split this into four words: trust, engagement, advocacy, and value. Let's explore.

Trust

Although not all aspects of a good customer relationship can be solved by technology, it should be noted that nearly half of the respondents in Forrester's April 2022 report on CDP owners stated that they expect increased trust from customers as a result of their investments in a modern, effective CDP.[145]

To support this idea, a 2021 study from Salesforce that surveyed nearly 17,000 consumers and business buyers reports that 52% of customers generally trust companies, up from 48% in their 2020 report.[146] It appears that increased investments are paying off, though this still means that nearly half of all consumers *don't* trust companies!

Engagement

An inactive relationship isn't much of a benefit to anyone involved. Thus, engagement is an important aspect of a customer relationship.

Customers who don't use a product or service, don't tell others about it, don't engage with it, or don't continue their subscriptions, upgrade, or buy new products when needed are valuable in that they are a one-time sale, but their LTV can't compare to a more engaged customer.

Likewise, engagement goes both ways. Brands that don't engage their customers by asking for feedback fail to provide methods of staying loyal or evangelizing about their products. They only have themselves to blame when a customer disengages. Of course, brands need to provide great products and good service, but beyond that, there needs to be more for a customer to do if they want to stay engaged. Building a House of the Customer provides a wealth of opportunities to engage with customers in a variety of ways across platforms and channels.

Advocacy

Advocacy takes engagement beyond the individual customer and translates to referrals, public posts on social media or other forums, and other methods of proactively promoting a brand, product, or service.

Although this can be done in exchange for favors or money, I'm not going to discuss that particular kind of advocacy here. Hiring influencers, public relations (PR) firms, or digital marketers can be done to effective results, but those individuals don't fall into this category of advocates.

What I mean by *advocacy* is unpaid and generally unsolicited promotion of a brand and its products and services. I say "generally" unsolicited because a brand may have a program that makes it easy to share feedback, reviews, thoughts, images, and so on, but they don't pay for this promotion.

Like engagement, advocacy goes both ways as well. Although customers who serve as advocates are often vocal about their love for brands, some of the best advocacy is more understated. In fact, if what seems like advocacy for customers ends up being more beneficial as a PR stunt, it's not really advocacy. Instead, brands need to make customers feel as though the brand is their advocate for no other reason than it is the right way to treat customers who support them.

Value

Last, but certainly not least, a good customer relationship creates *value* for both parties: brand and customer. If customers don't gain significant and consistent value from the relationship, they may move on to another brand or simply not come back.

Likewise, if a customer doesn't provide value to a brand, or if the brand isn't able to measure the value a customer creates, it's not a winning situation. Notice the second part of that caveat, however. In some cases, customers may be advocates for the brand while not spending as much as others deemed "high value" to the company.

Another thing to keep in mind is the Pareto principle, which states that approximately 80% of consequences originate from 20% of causes.[147] In the case of customers, it means that a particularly valuable customer segment making up only one-fifth of your customer population contributes to four-fifths of your sales, profits, or both. Keep this in mind when you are tempted to define an "average" customer, as well.

Measuring Customer Relationships

I cover this topic in much greater detail in my previous book, *Meaningful Measurement of the Customer Experience* (2022), so I will simply summarize here. Although there are many ways to measure CX, I have found that the best results come from measuring several dimensions while not overloading your team with numbers that can't be acted upon.

I recommend considering customer experience measurements using three main categories:

- Customer-facing (quantitative and qualitative)
- Internal-facing (product and process)
- Holistic (composite scores like engagement scores and measurement across the journey)

Your measurement of customer relationships then needs to be aligned and tied with your business outcome metrics.

2.6.2 Different Customers, Different Experiences

As much as companies try to provide great experiences, the "2022 Twilio State of Customer Engagement Report" states that while 75% of B2C companies surveyed say they provide good or excellent personalized experiences, only 48% of consumers say they receive good or excellent personalized brand experiences. Of even greater concern: 46% of consumers rate personalized experiences as merely "average."[148]

Considering the amount of competition out there, average isn't going to cut it. We need to not only provide great experiences but make it easy to stay loyal and tell others about our brands as well.

This is why it's critical to understand customers and what motivates them to share their feelings about a brand. We want them to become our evangelists. In Lacek Group and Sitecore's recent report, "The Changing Look of Loyalty," the top three reasons global respondents gave for why they would post, share, like, or review a brand on social media were

- To share a positive experience (54%)
- To share something new or interesting (47%)
- To promote a product they enjoy (46%)[149]

There are a few things to note about this. First, none of these items include a financial component (the fourth top answer did, however, mention finding a great deal). Second, notice that *experience* is first, and by a relatively wide margin. The other promising findings in this survey are that only 28% of respondents stated they would complain about a negative experience, and only 23% would complain about a bad product experience. Regardless of whether that holds up in a real-world setting, it is at least encouraging to know that respondents started from a place of positivity when thinking about sharing their feelings on a brand.

Let's briefly look at the types of customers that our House of the Customer needs to support (Figure 2.6.2.1):

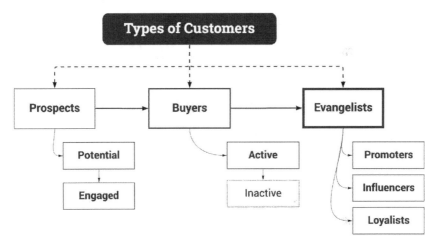

Figure 2.6.2.1, Types of Customers the House of the Customer Needs to Support

We've got three main categories: prospects who are researching and considering before a purchase, buyers who are customers who are buying or have bought the product or service, and evangelists who are customers and product users who share their experiences with others intentionally or passively. There are also several subtypes under each, but I want to focus on understanding the nuance of different customer evangelists, as I think these are the most in need of explanation. They are also, arguably, the most beneficial category when in holistic measurements like CLV.

The Three Types of Evangelists

Let's revisit Figure 2.6.2.1 and focus on the evangelists. In the last chapter, I talked about advocacy as an attribute of good customer relationships. I also mentioned that unpaid advocacy was a sign of a good relationship. As we look at evangelists, we're going to include individuals who aren't paid to promote as well as some who might be. Here are the three types of evangelists I've identified.

Promoters

These are customers who are vocal about their support for the brand. They recommend the company's products and services and even help potential customers decide what to buy. They aren't paid to promote the brand—it simply comes naturally. They want others to have the same great experience they've already had.

Influencers

Although promoters show their brand love with their words, influencers show their loyalty to a brand with their actions in test reviews, videos, and the like. Influencers are often paid for their reviews and mentions, though this is not always the case. Many thought leaders and influencers simply like brands or use brands as case studies of exemplary behavior.

Loyalists

Finally, we have what I call loyalists, who are the least public and vocal about their love of a brand, product, or service. But this doesn't make them any less loyal. These loyalists are not paid by a brand but instead buy, buy often, renew subscriptions, and so forth. Their friends, colleagues, and family might know about their loyalty, but these individuals aren't posting TikTok videos showing off their love of a brand.

Supporting Your Supporters

Of course, you and your team are going to want a thorough understanding of *all* your different customers. I recommend reviewing these categories and seeing if there are any missing, as well as clearly defining what each category of customer means to your audience segmentation and methods of defining customer groups.

This also means getting a good understanding of the type of content and experiences that these customer types need and desire. Chances are they're very different in some areas and similar in others. Your House of the Customer needs to accommodate a variety of customer content, journey stages, and personalized experiences based on how an individual wants to interact with your brand.

2.7 The Roof: Processes and Systems

The time to repair the roof is when the sun is shining.
—John F. Kennedy

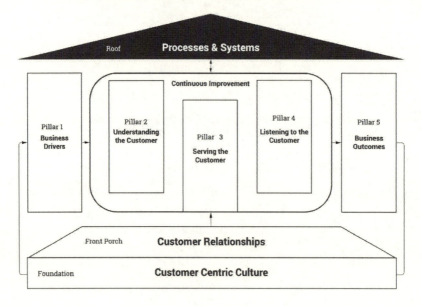

Figure 2.7.1, The Roof: Processes and Systems

As I mentioned in the introduction, our House of the Customer's roof provides all our protective systems and processes that allow our House to function properly. When done well, these not only provide stability and consistency, but allow for continual optimization and management of change over time.

North Star State

There are a few things to keep in mind when it comes to the roof; that is, the systems and processes that shelter our House of the Customer and ensure things run smoothly.

Although we want consistency in our processes, we also need alignment between several sometimes-chaotic elements. People, processes, and platforms are all subject to radical change and the need for reinterpretation.

System and process changes should always be addressed with employees. This means having transparency about how these processes function and why they are used. Additionally, we need systems and processes designed to adapt and change over time. As new information becomes available, consumer preferences change, and new ideas surface, we need to take what works and make it better.

This balance between stability and change is part of what makes agile approaches so attractive, and it's why I am a fan of implementing agile principles in my work.

What We Will Cover

In this section, we are going to talk about how critical alignment can be. We're going to talk about aligning people, processes, and platforms to generate the type of transformation that a House of the Customer creates. Then, we will look at the all-important feedback loop that enables continuous improvement using agile principles.

2.7.1 Aligning People, Processes, and Platforms

Transformation initiatives of many kinds are in progress across the business world, all intending to fix the challenges currently plaguing organizations. Unfortunately, there's rarely a silver bullet that can fix a challenge all by itself. Instead, solutions are often a combination of elements working together. For instance, have you ever overheard someone say, "Once we have [insert software product name] in place, everything will work better"?

Although software has a tremendous ability to affect change, it takes more than new technology to create positive change. In addition to furnishing technology solutions, we need to ensure the *people* using the technology and the *processes* that coordinate teams are also in place.

A little while back, I interviewed Sara Taheri, Vice President and Chief Platform Owner of Contact Center Transformation and Robotics at Prudential Financial, Inc., on *The Agile Brand Podcast*, and she shared the following:

> *People, processes, and platforms—also known as the three-legged stool! The combination of these three is balance. Technology is a key aspect of change and digital transformation, for sure. But without people and processes, sometimes digital transformations fall flat or don't have as much of an impact or adoption as they can. So as we are*

> *looking at transforming our technical stack, we need to look at and evaluate our processes and talent and make sure we evolve and show the proper attention in all three categories.*[150]

People

Improvements and changes in technology are often seen as complex components of a transformation or new initiative. However, securing buy-in from those affected by or responsible for that change can be the bigger challenge. It's important to plan for this from the beginning.

It is not enough to simply assume that employees will suddenly see the logic once a new system is in place and adapt without hesitation. There are good reasons for this.

First, there are reasons why current processes and platforms are being used in the first place. The way things are currently done is probably the result of some other change initiative years ago.

Second, changing someone's role can be daunting, even if it is a net improvement over their current status. What makes getting on board with change even more difficult is when employees aren't taught the reasons behind the change and have no say in its execution.

Empathizing with your team members and helping them understand the reasons for change can help ensure alignment and support from the start.

In my interview with Sara Taheri, she talked about the value of people in an organization:

> *People are our biggest assets. Ensuring we make it a priority to make sure they have the most up-to-date information so they can be successful in servicing our customers is really important. Our attention needs to be on looking at what we need to do to*

make their work lives easier. Ultimately happier customer service agents allow for better servicing and, as a result, better customers.

Aside from hiring, retention, and recognition programs, other things that come to mind include considering things like improving collaboration tools so reps can quickly communicate with peers so they can service the customer faster and efficiently, without long hold times, or improving knowledge-management tools or materials so the agent can find the information they need quickly to service customers.

These are examples of putting our agents first so they have the information and tools they need at their fingertips to provide the great service they want to provide to their customers.

Although technology can be expensive to procure and maintain, leaders shouldn't underestimate the cost of losing key team members. They not only retain internal knowledge but can coach new team members. Losing a key team member also means a disruption to the business while the role goes unfilled, as they often have during the Great Resignation.

Processes

Even if you've done the work of ensuring buy-in from your stakeholders and employees, it's impossible to achieve success if no one knows what they need to do or how to do it.

For instance, the perfect software solution could be available to your team, but if the appropriate operating procedures aren't also rolled out, that software may lie dormant, cause inefficiencies, or even create unhappy customers due to misunderstandings. This is why making training and support available to employees is key.

Creating strong processes also requires understanding how to translate metrics into priorities. Sarah Taheri added her perspective in my interview with her based on her work with the customer service and call center at Prudential:

> *We may want to consider evaluating our metrics and what we measure and determine if the organizational metrics require updating. Perhaps, at some point, an organization may have been focused on reducing the call handle time, and now it needs to be focused on reducing its call transfers. If that's the case, they should be thinking through what processes or trainings would need to change to reduce transferring a call. Maybe that is increasing our agent training so they can handle a multitude of call types.*

Finally, while it is important for people to understand *why* a change or transformation is needed, it is just as important that they understand *how* the new platform or tools will be used.

Platforms

A CleverTouch report shows that 44% of marketers surveyed said they have platforms that have gone largely unused during the pandemic, with 34% saying that they are at least not fully utilizing those platforms. Despite this, over a third say they still plan to buy more in the next twelve months![151] This gap between technology and how thoroughly it is used needs to be addressed.

It's not enough to just get one element of people, processes, and technology correct. All three elements need to be aligned to ensure both initial and long-term success. By keeping this in mind from the start of any initiative, you have the best chance of realizing the potential of your change or transformation initiative.

Next, we are going to explore how to ensure our people, processes, and platforms are not only aligned in the first place, but *stay* aligned. This will involve building feedback loops so we can better understand the opportunities and challenges to improvement.

2.7.2 The Feedback Loop

The benefits of a customer-centric approach are well-documented and understood. Improved customer experience and the processes and platforms involved benefit from this customer-centric approach and result in more long-term customer satisfaction, greater word-of-mouth reach, and in many cases, happier employees driven by a common purpose.

Although most organizations agree that customer centricity is important, they often differ on how they deliver that promise. Agile principles can play a key role in achieving sustainable growth and improvement in customer experience. This means that there are more gradual changes over time, but often there are more continuous changes taking place. In other words, the change may not ever really end! Although this may sound scary to some, it is the only way to ensure that people, processes, and platforms are continually performing at their best.

In my podcast interview with Sara Taheri, she shared the following:

> *With the shift to agile and iteratively adding value, agile teams work on implementing capabilities in an incremental fashion. We no longer live in a world where we turn off old processes one day and start on a new system with new processes the next. This means our old technology solutions and new platforms are sometimes working in parallel, and our people have to toggle or*

work in multiple environments as their technology solutions gradually shift into the new world.[152]

Let's dive in a little deeper to look at CX and continuous improvement and how they can work together for the benefit of the business, its customers, as well as its employees.

Continuous Improvement and Its Role in the Customer Experience

How are you testing and refining customer experiences once they're rolled out? It's not enough to create a good plan and then hope it won't ever need adjustment. To tie all this together, we need to create a system that allows us to test hypotheses about the customer experience, collect data, analyze it, and quickly make meaningful adjustments.

So how do we keep all of this organized and cohesive, both internally as an organization and externally to the customer? When I interviewed Sami Nuwar, CX Director at Medallia, he had the following to say:

> *I can answer that question with one word, and that's alignment. First of all, we align on our purpose like, Why do we exist? and What is the direction we intend to go? So let's align on that to make sure we're all on the same page. Then we also align just as I alluded to before. We align onto work that we are doing or intend to do across all business functions.*
>
> *We're so busy executing, but at the same time, we need to give ourselves permission to take a step back every once in a while to periodically and retrospectively assess our progress on a cross-functional on a cross-functional basis and understand what other areas are doing. It's hard to do that when you don't*

come together periodically and align on the work and make sure that that work aligns to the purpose so that we're all going in this in the same direction

It's just like a car. We're driving in our cars every day, and our North Star is guided by the steering wheel, and every once in a while we're going to hit a pothole, and you're going to see the car start to drift left or right, even though you point it in a certain direction. And that's why we take our cars in to get some maintenance done every three months, right? You have a schedule to take your car in to get your tires rotated and get a realignment, and that makes sure that the wheels of the car are pointed in a direction of the steering wheel. The business is no different than that.[153]

Agile principles recommend a system of continuous feedback, analysis, and improvement that leads to better outcomes for all involved. You might be familiar with the concept of sprints, which include sets of business outcomes and related requirements that are done over short periods of time. This sprint-based approach means that you have enough time to collect data, analyze it, and make meaningful improvements. Limiting yourself to only a few weeks also limits a project's ability to become unnecessarily large.

When you have a good feedback loop that allows you to determine where improvements should be made, you can then apply your methods to help prioritize what to do and when to do it. You will likely have a large backlog of items, but using the business value definition described earlier in this book will help ensure your process of continuous improvement works.

Don't Forget the Teams Doing the Work

Since the Great Resignation, we are seeing many team members leave jobs where they no longer feel fulfilled. This is causing disruptions both internally and externally, as customers often feel the downstream effects of teams that are short-staffed and short on morale.

Agile principles recommend that both employees and customers be valued over systems and tools. Because of this, your processes must take into account the people who will utilize them. Agile principles also put a strong focus on the democracy of ideas within a team. Although there is a product owner responsible for ensuring business value is delivered, how the work gets done is an open and collaborative process.

With so many employees struggling to find purpose in their work, approaches like this are one way to demonstrate how they provide individual value while simultaneously bringing them closer to their team members.

One important way to take care of your team members is through honesty and transparency. Sara Taheri shared the following in my interview with her:

> *It is important to be honest and transparent about all aspects of the initiative without hiding anything. I always want to hear from the team and know if they are confident in what they are taking on within a sprint or within a quarterly program increment. If not, we discuss it.*
>
> *Another effective strategy is being open to respectfully challenging one another. There is something to be said when someone speaks up and provides a differing idea or opinion. Just the idea of raising a point gets the creative juices flowing,*

and next thing you know, you are either on board and making a change or getting more creative in how you are solving for it.[154]

All of that together has the potential to increase both individual and team morale, while aligning everyone to provide the best customer experience.

As you can see, using agile principles and methods to guide your customer experience initiatives can have winning results for both customers and the employees who serve them. Your organization's interpretation of agile may vary, but the most important thing you can do is adhere to a set of principles that guide your work into the future.

We've now completed reviewing all the elements of our House of the Customer. You could say we took a full tour of the house! Now we're going to explore how to go about building your own House of the Customer, with several things to keep in mind as you do so.

Part 3: Building the House

We shape our buildings; thereafter, they shape us.
—Winston Churchill

In 1884, Sarah Winchester, newly widowed and having recently lost her infant daughter, made a decision to leave her home in New Haven, Connecticut, and head west. Sarah's late husband was William Wirt Winchester, who left her a 50% stake in his firearms company and the fortune it provided when he passed away.

Sarah purchased a lot in San Jose, California, and proceeded to build what would become one of the most fascinating homes in history. With no blueprints and a seemingly inexhaustible supply of cash, Sarah Winchester provided day-to-day guidance over what would become a seven-story house with 161 rooms, 47 fireplaces, ten thousand panes of glass, two basements, three elevators, hidden rooms, and more.[155]

Her motivation to build in this manner is debated, but many consider it to be inspired by her consultations with a medium following her husband's and daughter's untimely deaths. The medium, supposedly channeling the spirit of her late husband, said she must continuously build a home for herself and the victims of Winchester firearms.[156] The medium claimed the house needed intentionally confusing details, such as stairs leading nowhere, doors opening to solid walls, and bathrooms whose plumbing didn't work (to prevent the haunting of faucets).

Construction on the house occurred without interruption, with carpenters working around the clock from sometime in 1884 to Sarah Winchester's death on September 5, 1922.[157] Despite having many features that were rare for the time, such as hot running water and push-button gas lighting, the house was practically unusable for the most part. Although certain rooms and areas could function, the staircases to nowhere, nonworking bathrooms, and other "features" created to prevent ghosts from disturbing its inhabitants meant that this sprawling house was nothing more than a novelty.

Although your digital transformation won't literally have stairs to nowhere, can you empathize with some of this? Surely you've seen a few *metaphorical* stairs to nowhere appear, whether they are new products that popped up or software platforms that were purchased but never fully utilized.

Additionally, how important is it that the team stays busy, even when there isn't clear direction on what needs to be built, how, and why? Is there a culture of busywork that prioritizes doing over strategy? Is there simply not a clear understanding of why teams are doing what they are doing? What about all the technical debt that accrues when work that isn't future-proof requires rework?

Perhaps Sarah Winchester looks more and more like a leader you've known or worked with in the past! Although I hope not, I'm sure you can see some parallels.

What We Will Cover

We're going to talk about how to get started building your own House of the Customer.

We're going to explore a few key areas in this section that are critical to success. We'll start with covering people, processes, and platforms—the "three-legged stool." Then we'll talk about not only where to start, but how to sustain and improve efforts already in progress.

Let's begin this final section of the book!

3.1 People

We are what we repeatedly do. Excellence, then, is not an act, but a habit.
—Aristotle

Brands know that customers want personalized experiences but often fail to connect the dots between personalization and end-result impact on the bottom line. This leads to embarking on long-term digital transformation initiatives that may fail to hit the mark. According to a 2020 survey by Boston Consulting Group, 70% of digital transformations fail or fall short of their objectives, and the ones that succeed create 66% more value on average, improve internal capabilities by 82%, and significantly impact customer experience and the bottom line.[158]

To be one of those successful organizations means to either close the competitive gap or pull into a leadership position in a category. This requires providing customer experiences that are personalized and optimized.

To do this, brands need to approach personalization and personalized content in a way that is:

- Cost-effective (i.e., it can be achieved operationally without being overly burdensome on content creators)
- Measurable (i.e., testing and optimization are clearly defined)
- Achieves the desired business results

Yet the road to personalized omnichannel customer experiences can be long and treacherous if you don't have a good plan. Keeping the components of the House of the Customer in mind is a great way to start. It is also important to be realistic about both the internal and external barriers to success.

We're going to start examining how to build our House of the Customer alongside the people—employees and other team members—who do the important work of planning, building, and implementing. Although there is a lot of talk about employee engagement (there are many great books on that topic), I still feel there is a disconnect.

Employee engagement and leadership best practices are too often looked at in the abstract, so when the need for practical application arises, it feels difficult to reconcile. For instance, if 70% of digital transformations fail as previously mentioned, there clearly is a disconnect. Are all of those companies terrible places to work? Do all of them fail their employee-engagement surveys?

I think the *people* part of the three-legged stool of people, processes, and platforms is the most overlooked of all, though *processes* isn't far behind.

Let's start by talking about the people involved in building your House of the Customer and look at several ways to be more successful. These are based on my firsthand experience as well as talking and working with many experts in the field.

Resistance to Change

The first aspect of change I want to discuss is the *resistance* to it. It's natural to be comfortable in our lives and work once we find a flow that suits us. Even if you don't love your job, you have most likely found a way to create routines, shortcuts, and other methods to get your work done as easily as possible.

When a large initiative or transformation is presented, there are likely to be many who are less than thrilled about their lives changing. There are many reasons for this, including the concept of absorption that we discussed earlier in the customer-centric culture chapter.

Here, though, I want to discuss the concept of resistance to change so we can better understand and deal with it. According to an article by Kirti Sharma, five common reasons cause employees resistance to change:[159]

- *Mistrust and lack of confidence.* Employees don't trust that their leaders know what is best, nor do they trust that leadership understands the impact that large-scale changes will have on their day-to-day responsibilities.
- *Emotional responses.* These include natural reactions to a perceived threat to the status quo—whether that implies a need to retrain, upskill to remain in a position, take on more work, or face other reasonable concerns in the face of change.
- *Fear of failure.* This means that the individual fears they aren't up to the task or will be unable to learn the skills necessary to adopt change.
  Similarly, since so many digital transformations fail to meet their objectives, there can be fear that a failed transformation might mean cutbacks or job losses.
- *Poor communication.* "We know that things are changing, but we're not sure exactly what is changing, nor do we know when it is happening." Ever heard something like that? If you have, you've got a problem. Resistance to change is exacerbated by unclear deadlines, goals, and communication with employees.

- *Unrealistic timelines.* With increasing competition and consumer demand, why wouldn't you want your digital transformation to be complete as soon as possible? One good reason is that the people implementing the change are going to resist! And with good reason. These are the people keeping the company running, customers happy, and current systems functioning. Finding an iterative, agile approach to implementing change can alleviate pressure.

The Kübler-Ross Change Curve

Before we further examine emotional responses to change, let's work through the steps of the Kübler-Ross change curve, also known as the five stages of grief.[160] Yes, it sounds a bit dramatic for a discussion on digital transformation, but it has been successfully and rather broadly applied to organizational and other personal change since its inception.[161]

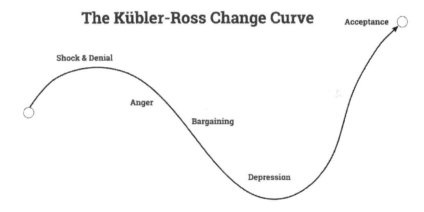

Figure 3.1.1, The Kübler-Ross Change Curve

As you can see in the figure above (Figure 3.1.1) we ultimately reach acceptance after a series of steps:

1. Shock and denial

2. Anger
3. Bargaining
4. Depression
5. Acceptance

A good manager and leader knows you can't really skip a step here, but the goal instead is to understand that big changes aren't easy for anyone. The best way to help with this is to look at ways to manage resistance to change, which we'll discuss next.

Ways to Manage Resistance to Change

Now that we've explored the symptoms of resistance to change, let's explore what to do about it!

Executive and Stakeholder Buy-In

I've said this in different ways, both in this book as well as in my other writings: nothing happens without stakeholder support. If you are trying to overcome an obstacle and create transformation in your organization, you need executives and leaders that have your back—not just in words, but in actions. I can't stress this enough.

Just as important as stakeholder support is the need for a clear, consistent message that change is needed and for good reasons. When I talked with Alex Atzberger, CEO of Optimizely, on *The Agile Brand* podcast, he described it like this:

> *For me, it always comes back to this notion of, do you have enough urgency and enough resolve inside the organization to actually drive [the] effort? Ultimately you need to build the*

case for change. It starts with understanding your customer and where they go to buy.[162]

Transparent Communication

The urgency talked about above needs to come from clear, consistent communication, and allow team members to maximize their buy-in, engagement, and constructive participation at the right time. Here are three rules to follow to be successful in this.

Rule 1: Be Transparent about Goals and Expectations, and Provide Regular Progress Updates

People are a lot more open to making change happen when you let them in on the bigger picture. Don't mistake this for asking them for permission to set the goals to whatever you need them to be. Instead, as a leader, it is your job to share the vision and paint a clear-enough picture with words, charts, and other means so they can both get excited about the result, as well as help you fill in details along the way. Also, make sure to keep everyone informed. A large-scale initiative involves many moving pieces across many teams, and it will help to share what other teams are doing to contribute to the overall picture.

Rule 2: Get Team Members at All Levels Involved Early On

It is much easier to get buy-in from even skeptical employees if you involve them early on and make them part of the solution. If you don't, you're going to have to convince those same reluctant people to get on board with an idea they had no part in shaping. In my experience, the latter is an uphill climb, to say the least. Remember, you don't have to ask for input on everything, but allowing employees to shape aspects of transformation that directly impact their day-to-day roles can be beneficial. It may even circumvent issues that others were unable to foresee.

Rule 3: Be Open to Changing or Modifying Approaches to Achieve the Goal

Being a leader in the age of agile business means being flexible and adaptive while staying true to a goal. Your job as a leader is less about always having the right answers and more about knowing how to listen to the best ideas that help you achieve your strategic vision. For example, Filippo Catalano, CIO of Nestle and one of the leaders behind the organization's InGenius innovation accelerator says, "You want to encourage people to be curious, innovative, courageous, and collaborative. This means also empowering our employees and harnessing their passion and knowledge to bring innovation to the company."[163]

Cross-Team Collaboration

A big challenge within any organization is siloing—of teams, roles, and responsibilities—despite being engaged in a large-scale initiative. If you doing something like building your own House of the Customer or other digital transformation initiative, however, this can often exacerbate any existing friction between teams.

Teams may have differing priorities, timelines, KPIs, and even ways of describing customers and their challenges. Similar to what I said about managing resistance to change, encouraging cross-team collaboration requires clear, transparent communication of expectations. It also requires building teams comprised of cross-disciplinary team members to encourage a greater understanding of the necessary pieces when building a customer-centric platform.

What makes a high-performing team? For that, I turn to John Estafanous, Founder and CEO of Rallybright, a platform developed by behavioral scientists, organizational development psychologists, and others that measures team performance. Here's what he said when I interviewed him for *The Agile Brand Podcast*:

> *We use resilience as one of the key barometers for what drives a high-performance team. So when we think of resilience, we think about being able to engage with adversity, to sustain performance through adversity, and as you overcome obstacles, to rebound from setbacks and then learn and grow from the experience.*
>
> *So that's how we would define a high-performing team. . . . It's a team that's able to stay together, stay on mission, stay on target, and work through any of the challenges that are presented to them. And not only work through them but thrive through them, to some degree, and ultimately learn and grow from those experiences. And when you have teams that do that, it's something really special.*[164]

We'll talk more about some ways to solve this in more detail in the "Continuing to Build" chapter.

Time and Resource Requirements

It probably goes without saying, but creating the number of variations required for personalized content takes more time and effort than less sophisticated options (Figure 3.1.2). Think about it. If you are usually creating one or two variations, then start personalizing by even four or five segments, you are going to increase production time considerably.

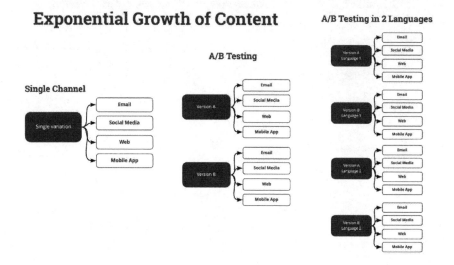

Figure 3.1.2, Exponential Growth of Content Management Needs

If you continue to do A/B testing, you'll go from two variations to eight or ten in that scenario. Even with automated methods of generating content variations, more effort will still be required. Now consider an organization that needs content in more than one language. This means that each of your A and B tests now needs at least two variations, one for each language. If you are a fully global organization, the number of country-language combinations needed can exceed forty.

This means more time for content writers and graphic designers to create content, more time for the data team to identify the proper audience segments, and more time for the marketing team to set up additional tests and variations.

According to recent research by Optimizely, 75% of business executives surveyed believe their organization is generating good content that's being poorly leveraged.[165] Here's what Alex Atzberger, CEO of Optimizely, had to say about this:

> *[Creating great content] is a big challenge that a lot of companies have. [Optimizely believes] that you are what you read, what content you look at, what podcasts you listen to. One of the things that I found most helpful for companies was a very simple view of their content, and it's basically a matrix where on one side we say, "What content do you publish?" and then on the other side as of the matrix is "What content do people read?" What you basically see is how much content have you published on a certain given topic versus [what] your prospects or customers are reading.*
>
> *So, you start to get analytical and data-driven around your content production and what people are actually interested in. We do this for companies that sometimes have hundreds of thousands of pages of content. There's a massive amount of content out there, and they suddenly recognize they did not know certain topics were in such high demand, yet they have so little content on those.[166]*

There are ways to streamline solutions to these challenges, but you need to plan accordingly. Automation can play a strong role here, as can strategically outsourcing repetitive tasks or translation work.

Leaders should be clear in their communication that they are both aware of these challenges and open to all good solutions. They should show their commitment by making smart investments in solutions that will improve the teams' ability to scale their content creation.

Although your organization may have its own unique challenges and opportunities to explore, keeping these items in mind will help as you embark on change initiatives. Next, we're going to explore things to keep in mind when developing or modifying your processes, which are often closely aligned with how your people do their work and communicate.

3.2 Processes

You can use an eraser on the drafting table or a sledgehammer on the construction site.
—Frank Lloyd Wright

"Let's not reinvent the wheel." How many times have you heard that phrase in your career? I feel like I hear it several times a month, if not a week. Well, I'm here to tell you sometimes it is beneficial to rethink your tried-and-true methods, but even changing processes requires processes of their own. There are several reasons for this.

Although no one wants to be part of something that's inefficient, we also seek stability in our work, and (as discussed in the last chapter) are resistant to change—particularly when that change doesn't have a strong purpose behind it.

Also, no one wants to try to follow a process that hasn't been thought through from start to finish. Employees balk when they feel as though orders have been "handed down" to them without any empathy or understanding of what it actually takes to do the work. In a recent webinar for Medallia, Michelle Peluso, chief customer officer at CVS, shared a compelling method that keeps leadership grounded in understanding what their frontline employees' jobs are like:

> At CVS, our leadership each do different jobs regularly. We work in the store, stock trucks, work in the pharmacy, or do inventory tax price changes. Then we come back together and

have a two-hour deep dive. It is amazing how much you realize you can do to make the experience for that colleague better when you experience it firsthand.[167]

Couldn't agree more, Michelle! Walking in the shoes of your employees is a process that leadership needs to consider as soon as possible.

Let's look at some of the other ways that process helps us as we build our House of the Customer.

Start with an Agile Mindset

Managing the type of change often required to create a House of the Customer requires people, processes, and platforms to work together in harmony. It also requires that the organization adapt and adjust using the best information and approaches available. This is where agile approaches complement transformation and change initiatives very well.

Marketers and CX professionals face increasing pressure to provide the most relevant content, offers, and experiences. The competition only seems to increase as consumers have more options to choose from, some of which are available instantly or at least overnight.

To keep up with these demands, teams must become more agile, which includes reimagining how success is defined and measured as well as how to approach continuous improvement. Agile principles can and have helped many teams and organizations achieve these goals.

Chris Worle—fintech adviser, investor, and former chief digital officer at Hargreaves Landsdown—has this to say about the need for an agile mindset in organizations:

With digital transformation, people almost have in their minds that there's going to be some sort of ribbon-cutting ceremony one day, and everything will become easier and faster. That's not the way transformation is. Many businesses have catching up to do from the point of view of technology, of culture, of organizational design, but transformation and the digital way of working now is about getting a business to a point where it can continue to adapt, evolve, and work in an agile manner.[168]

Continuous Improvement

For those familiar with agile practices, this may seem redundant, but I want to highlight that processes that emphasize continuous improvement are vital to building and optimizing your House of the Customer.

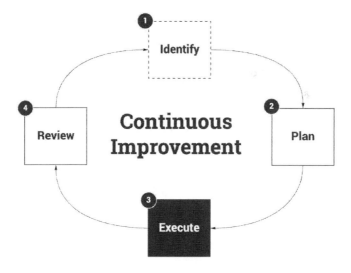

Figure 3.2.1, Continuous Improvement

Although continuous improvement can also be a *mindset*, it works much better if it is a more formalized process with these four steps (Figure 3.2.1):

1. Identify
2. Plan
3. Execute
4. Review

If you are also using agile practices, these steps closely align with a scrum approach. Even if you aren't, these four steps can be used to ensure you're methodically incorporating successes into subsequent iterations and not repeating costly mistakes or errors.

The Journey Is the Blueprint

As we saw previously in this book when discussing measurement, customer journey maps are vital to understanding important internal gaps and opportunities to improve the customer experience. They also never fail to highlight important areas, no matter how familiar you think you are with the customer experience and internal processes that support it. If you haven't mapped the customer journey, you should do so as soon as is feasible.

If you have created a customer journey map for one purpose or another, have you included personalization considerations as well?

Doing so will allow you to better understand key moments when personalized content will be of the greatest value.

As you map the customer journey to create personalized experiences, be sure to do the following:

- Consider the data you have on a customer at that point in the journey. Is it enough to personalize?

- Look for areas where multichannel personalization opportunities would benefit the customer.
- Understand which platforms will need to be collected to personalize the experience.
- Be mindful of the teams and processes needed to create the content variations necessary to personalize each moment the customer engages with your channels.
- Consider how you'll perform multivariate testing and analysis, and determine what success looks like.

There are many ways to map a customer journey, but given the amount of detail you need to collect, I strongly recommend using a collaborative digital tool such as an interactive Miro Board, or even a Google spreadsheet. This can make it easier to ensure thoroughness in addition to getting ideas and insights from everyone involved.

Taxonomy: A Common Language

As we explored during the components of a House of the Customer, there are numerous data sets, internal and external systems and platforms, as well as people and processes that need to work together to create the optimal personalized experience across the customer journey.

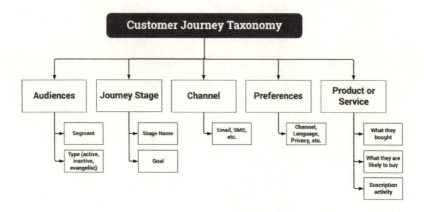

Figure 3.2.2, Customer Journey Taxonomy

This means that a common language must be established (Figure 3.2.2) to ensure that when a piece of content is created, the teams doing so can answer these questions:

- Who is the customer?
- What product or service do they already own or are interested in buying?
- What stage of the customer journey are they in?
- What channel are they using, or which channel would they prefer?
- What language do they speak?

And so on.

Taxonomy, or the science of classification, has origins as far back as the advent of human language, though its modern form was created by Swedish botanist Carl Linnaeus in 1758 to classify species of plants and animals.[169] The Linnean system, in which each species of animal or plant receives a name with two terms, where the first identifies the genus and the second the species itself, improved upon previous iterations evolved from the Greeks and Romans.[170]

More recently, taxonomy has been used in other domains, including technology, to classify all manner of things. This includes content to be served to customers via marketing technology platforms and is the reason why taxonomy is part of our discussion on building a House of the Customer.

Why a Customer Journey Taxonomy Is Important

Because so much information is needed to understand a customer's journey, it is important to establish a taxonomy so that content creators use the same categories as marketers setting up automation in an email platform and data scientists setting up a CDP.

As we explore some of the challenges of creating personalized omnichannel customer experiences in the next chapter, you'll see even more examples of how a customer journey taxonomy can be useful, if not downright critical.

Make sure you involve team members across disciplines when creating a taxonomy so that you build a complete picture that includes the following:

- Definitions of journeys and journey stages
- Content types
- Data sets needed for customers, products, and services
- Desired actions
- Channel-specific information
- Tracking information
- Data privacy, localization, and compliance information

Of course, the above is just a partial list. Depending on how many channels you utilize and the methods of orchestration, this taxonomy can be quite robust, even as a starting point.

Although your taxonomy will grow alongside your needs, take time to think ahead as much as you can. Although adding subcategories down the line may be straightforward, making more fundamental changes can have a substantial impact that causes costly or time-consuming modifications to multiple systems and processes.

Moving toward Omnichannel Personalization

You don't have to start with omnichannel personalization. Instead, you can begin adding one channel at a time (Figure 3.2.3).

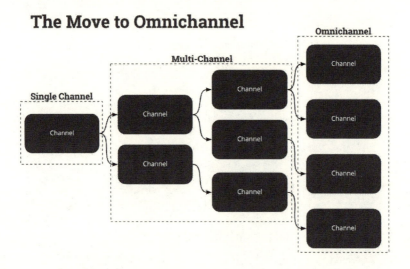

Figure 3.2.3, The Move to Omnichannel

For instance, maybe your website already offers personalization features, allowing you to connect your CDP and your email marketing to it. Then, shortly after that, you can add your social advertising or mobile app to the mix. By going one channel at a time, you can build a robust multichannel personalization program.

Content-Creation Process

Although many organizations are focused on the technology enabling multichannel personalization, the time and resources it takes to create content variations can slip through the cracks during planning.

As I mentioned earlier regarding common pain points, not having a streamlined content-creation process will seriously hinder your organization's ability to scale in the way that multichannel personalization across multiple audience segments demands.

Take the time to investigate improvements in your workflow and processes, including

- How multiple variations of images and copy will be sourced
- How the legal and compliance approval processes will be impacted
- How content will be managed, edited, and versioned
- How feedback about the content and process will be incorporated

By taking these and other issues into account, you can anticipate and get ahead of potential bottlenecks when it comes to content creation as your personalization efforts grow in sophistication.

Plant Your Brand Garden

What house wouldn't benefit from a nice garden? Our House of the Customer sure could. Remember the multiple reasons you want to collect both first- and zero-party data from your customers? When you get this information directly from your customers, you can offer them more personalized experiences, which translates into a great CLV.

To do this, you need to build a (virtual) place where customers can feel comfortable sharing information with the promise of receiving better or more relevant offers, discounts, increased access, and so on.

Many brands have taken approaches such as developing subscription models, publishing content as if they were a magazine, creating customer loyalty programs, and offering membership programs with advanced access to products and offers.

There are many different approaches you can take with this, and not every approach makes sense for every brand. Make sure you pick methods that create a seamless and logical customer experience rather than trying to force a first-person customer data strategy on customers that just don't see your brand the way you want them to.

Data Collection

Even with the best possible infrastructure and marketing strategies in place, if you don't have enough information about your customers and can't get new customers to provide meaningful data about themselves, your personalization efforts will be stunted.

This becomes even more important with the shift away from third-party cookie usage and support.

How to Manage Data-Collection Challenges

Try some of the following ideas to gather customer information for better personalization:

- Contests
- Gated content
- Offers

- Gamification
- Membership
- Loyalty programs
- Asking for small amounts of information over time

Customer Communities

Some brands have been using tactics to build their customer audiences for years. Many common approaches include customer loyalty programs or user communities. The obvious goal behind these and other similar programs is to build loyalty to both the brand and (in some cases) among other loyal users of a product or service. The added benefit for the brand is more willingness from their customers to share information about usage, personal information, and other data.

The *reason* sharing more information feels more palatable to customers is that they can see a direct correlation between providing information and the benefits they receive. Whether those benefits are points used in a reward system or better recommendations that help them use products or services more effectively, they feel a direct impact that makes sharing information acceptable.

Due to increasing restrictions on data privacy and third-party data usage, many brands that previously lacked direct relationships with their customers are exploring this area with subscription services and loyalty programs of their own. This is particularly true in the consumer-packaged goods space and other areas that primarily reached customers through intermediaries like big-box stores for retail or third-party data sources for advertising.

Governance

Last but not least, let's talk about governance. We discussed data governance in an earlier chapter, but here I want to touch on the governance of the entire House of the Customer.

For this, I'm going to turn to a conversation I had with Wendy Pravda, Principal Customer Experience advisor at Medallia. We talked specifically about CX governance, but what she said can apply to the broader governance needed for your House of the Customer. This is how she describes centralized, decentralized, and hybrid models of governance:

> *Centralized is when you have one CX organization with a single central leader. Picture one leader at the top, and there's strong corporate authority there. There's support from champions and key functions. I've really found that this model works best for smaller organizations. It could work for larger companies, but this is really a model where you have that central leadership, so that means it's going to be more autocratic in nature.*
>
> *Decentralized is different in that the CX program owners are in each business unit. So, think of multiple executives. There are independent CX teams and each department has autonomy, so that would work well in an organization that has multiple executive leaders or different sorts of businesses.*
>
> *Lastly, hybrid is the one, by far, that we recommend the most. It works well for a lot of companies. It's a blend of the two. There's a central advisory and governance with localized accountability. You have a team and councils that meet regularly, so those councils are made up of different people in the organization that meet. But you also have the individual*

> *teams focused on specific areas. The centralized corporate team focuses on methodology, systems, and best practices, and then the execution is done in the business units. So, it's the best of both worlds, and it can work for small or large organizations equally well.*[171]

We're going to return to that hybrid model in a couple of chapters as we discuss methods of continuing to build your House of the Customer. These methods include creating steering committees, working groups, or a Center of Excellence.

Conclusion

As you can see, there are many approaches to consider as you get started building your House of the Customer. Work with your team and stakeholders to find the best ways to get the maximum return in the shortest amount of time and with the lowest effort. You want to make sure you can prove the model that personalization brings a higher return before making larger time and resource investments.

3.3 Platforms

If art interprets our dreams, the computer executes them in the guise of programs!
—Alan Perlis

Earlier in the book, we talked about the types of platforms needed for data collection, serving the customer, and measurement. I won't be going through those again, but I am going to discuss different platform *approaches* and some of the pros and cons of each.

Moving from Legacy Infrastructure to a Future State

Let's revisit the resistance to change, as discussed in 3.1. As with any kind of change, people often resist adopting new platforms, infrastructure, and systems changes needed to make big changes happen.

One example of this is the adoption of cloud computing. Back in 2010, this was a $25 billion market, but by 2020, it had grown by 535%. Cloud computing adoption increased again in 2021 by over 35%.[172] I'm sure there were skeptics—"voices of reason"—that gave reasonable-sounding arguments along the way for why it wasn't time to change just yet. They did this even while 80% of companies were reporting operational improvements[173] and 82% of small and medium businesses report reduced costs after adopting cloud technology.[174]

Similarly, we've discussed a lot of platforms and approaches that require changes to successfully build a House of the Customer. These changes take a clear set of business objectives, measurable goals, and leadership support to happen. There will be inevitable missteps and difficulties along the way, but if you learn from these hiccups, the organization can still benefit.

Monolithic versus Best of Breed

First, some definitions. By *monolithic*, I mean broad, overarching systems with many features and components that work best when you buy more and more of those components.

By contrast, the *best-of-breed approach* refers to purchasing only the top-rated or best-matched platform or system in each category.

You might think from the subheading that I have a particular stance on this topic, but you'd be wrong! There are so many dependencies that can go into deciding to go one way or another. For instance, while a best-of-breed approach can get an organization some amazing features, you'll need more resources to integrate those systems compared to an all-in-one system.

Time to value is another key consideration, but this can go both ways. Large monolithic systems can sometimes create a quicker time-to-value turnaround than multiple systems working together. However, in some cases, an enterprise that turns on single systems one at a time takes a more iterative approach and thus decreases time to value.

So you can see that there is no one right answer here, but your strategy needs to take multiple elements into account.

Build versus Buy

Some organizations with more robust engineering teams decide to build some of the pieces needed for personalization instead of buying them off the shelf.

There are many reasons why building some (though generally not all) components makes sense, though there are also potential drawbacks, as you can see from the chart below (Figure 3.3.1):

Build

Pros
- The platform can be designed to do exactly what is needed for the systems you want to integrate.
- Data ownership, usage, consent, and privacy can sometimes be more tightly managed.

Cons
- Time to value can be longer than off-the-shelf options.
- Building a platform makes it difficult and costly to maintain integrations with multiple changing APIs.
- A custom platform usually doesn't have a common API language.

Buy

Pros

- The time to value is generally shorter.
- Integrations are often easier to implement thanks to many out-of-the-box API connectors.
- Packaged systems require less upkeep and have lower maintenance costs.

Cons

- You have less influence on the product roadmap and priorities.
- A monolithic system's features may or may not work out of the box with all your internal systems.
- Switching between monolithic platforms down the road can incur considerable costs.

Figure 3.3.1, Build versus Buy Comparison

Although building some components may provide a more tailored result, an organization needs to carefully weigh the benefits and drawbacks, sometimes on a per-component basis.

According to a recent survey by MarTech, the "buy" mentality is more prevalent than "build" at the moment. Their survey done in 2022 shows that only 11% of respondents replaced an existing commercial platform with a homegrown one, down from 13% in 2021. On the flip side, more than 25% of the respondents indicated that they replaced a homegrown system with a commercial one, which increased by 10% from the previous year.[175] The biggest reason for the replacements was better features offered by a software-as-a-service platform (53%), followed by the need to reduce the difficulty of integrating with other systems (16%).

A Hybrid Approach: Composable Platforms

There is another set of tools that can sometimes fit between the larger monolithic platforms and a build-it-yourself approach. These are what many call *composable platforms*, which have the benefits of a solid platform with API integrations and cloud-based delivery services. Although they often have robust features, they also allow brands to integrate their services with larger applications and may combine several tools together.

To learn a little more about this composable approach, I talked with Jason McClelland when he was Chief Marketing Officer at Algolia, a search platform with integrations for many e-commerce sites and far-reaching platforms like Nintendo Switch, Playstation, and NBC's The Voice app. I asked Jason how this approach can, in some cases, meet growing customer expectations:

> *Number one is setting the expectation with your vendors that this near real time is what you're looking for. Historically I don't know that people have known what to ask for or to know that they should have to set this expectation.*
>
> *Number two is it's getting easier and harder. The part that's getting easier is that in the past you had to build everything yourself. That's incredibly hard, and a multiyear process. Or it was hard because you're buying some monolithic off-the-shelf SaaS provider, and you're having to rip it apart to figure out,*

like, How exactly do I integrate it with my ERP? or How exactly do I integrate it with my PAM? How exactly do I integrate it with like my last mile customer experience, or the display layer? So that was really hard because essentially, you're fighting the system because the SaaS providers always pride themselves [on the fact] that you get the benefit of multitenant SaaS. It's like living in the same apartment as everyone else— you don't have to pay for your own plumbing, and that's true. The downside, then, is your apartment looks like everybody else's apartment because you're buying the same thing.

And if you're Dior, and you're trying to look different than, say, Loreal or some other premium brand, that's really hard when you're fighting the system and going, "Okay, we bought the same thing. How do we look different?" So it's gotten easier because there's been this rise of what Gartner calls composable software—companies like [Algolia] or Twilio or Stripe, which are bigger than an API and smaller than hosted SaaS. It's kind of like prebuilt LEGO blocks that make it easier for developers to build these experiences. So that part's gotten a lot easier from a build standpoint.

The part that's gotten a lot more complex is that, in the past, you would just ring up Salesforce, or you'd ring up Adobe, and you'd say, "Hey, I need a marketing system," and they'd say, "Hey, we got seven clouds. You know we're more than happy to sell you our seven clouds now." What you do is you call up Salesforce or Adobe, and you say, "Hey I need your content management system, but I'm going to go to these other composable companies and build a sort of experience layer around it." That's confusing, especially for marketing and business execs. You don't come from a technology background, and so part of the challenge of my job is explaining this.

As your go-to markets become more technical, you have businesspeople who come up through brand or demand or product marketing or product management and now suddenly, they're having to figure out APIs and composable and how [to] speak to [their] developer. There's a lot of work to do there, and there's a lot of gray area in the market because of that.[176]

So, as you can see, it is not necessarily as binary as "build" or "buy" in all cases. Composable platforms offer a hybrid approach.

Other Platform Challenges to Consider

I've touched on these in detail earlier in this book, so I'm just going to provide a short list here. The following are essential items for your House of the Customer and are all related to platform decisions:

- Unified customer profiles and IDs
- First-party customer data collection and storage
- Multi-touch attribution
- Orchestration and next best action across multiple channels
- Artificial intelligence and machine learning used in a beneficial and transparent way
- Measurement and reporting across the enterprise

These platform challenges and more await. But with a strong strategy, team alignment, and an agile, continuous-improvement approach, they will come together to create a well-functioning system that is customer-centric and tied to your business outcomes. Your House of the Customer awaits.

3.4 Continuing to Build

Success is the good fortune that comes from aspiration, desperation, perspiration and inspiration.
—Evan Esar

To continue building a house, we need to plan for the right tools to maintain it, right? All the electrical, plumbing, roofing, and other infrastructure elements need maintenance, not to mention the other appliances and internal fixtures. That isn't even considering the need for stylistic updates based on the latest trends and tastes. Our House of the Customer needs the same type of care, lest it become the haunted, abandoned house at the end of the street! Okay, maybe the "haunted" part is a little far-fetched, but I think you know what I mean.

A key decision you'll need to make is determining how extensive your transformation will be. Regardless of your organizational maturity, your business outcomes, and your customer satisfaction, staying competitive takes work. In my interview on *The Agile Brand* with Paulette Chafe of Zendesk, she shared three things to keep in mind as you begin:

First, things just don't magically happen or fall into place. They need to start to develop a roadmap for CX in their business. They need to start to plan it out and think about the experiences that they want to give today, twelve months from now, and twenty-four months from now. It is surprising the number of businesses who have taken a very ad-hoc approach toward CX and their planning. And I don't think that's going to give you the best results longer term. You know, there has to be some flexibility because new things pop up—new experiences are created. You need to be able to build that in. But I think sitting down and sort of plotting out walking a mile in the consumer's shoes and what the business can do to help that over a period will be beneficial.

They also need to challenge themselves on the metrics they use for measuring customer experience and customer service. A lot of businesses just use metrics like NPS or CSAT as numbers on a piece of paper. What we have seen is that the C-suite is now beginning to connect their performance remuneration against customer service metrics. So you really want to be vested in what you're doing and have some skin in the game.

The third area is they need to look at how they're funding their customer service and customer experience budgets. Our data has shown that funding is trailing behind volume and demand. And unless they fund this adequately going forward, how can they continue to exceed those expectations? Because, as demand rises, and has risen today, it's going to continue to grow even more, and so they do need to take a good, hard look at their funding, [and] as they start to build out their plans, . . .

> *say, "Are they giving it enough?" What they did last year is not going to be sufficient to meet the demands of next year.*[177]

Let's begin this chapter by exploring how we decide where to get started.

Where to Start: A Prioritization Model

If you were asked for all the ways you could improve the customer experience your organization delivers, how long would that list be? Whether it is five items or five hundred, you will need a way to prioritize your efforts sooner rather than later, or else you will be deadlocked by an overflowing list of "high-priority" items.

Agile principles recommend that features be prioritized by the business value they create. In this case, business value can take the form of two things: (1) efficiency and satisfaction from the employees maintaining and improving the products and (2) customer satisfaction when they use the products themselves.

Although there is healthy debate over how exactly to determine business value within an organization, you can decide how to do this based on your organization's strategic, customer, and financial goals. Your definition of *business value* may even evolve over time, which is fine as long as it is communicated to the teams involved.

The important thing to note is that a reliable, realistic prioritization method can be hugely helpful here. There are many ways to do this, including simple calculations that incorporate things like potential audience reach combined with the level of effort required. These can take the form of a simple spreadsheet with calculations or get more complex by tying in KPIs and calculations. How you approach it will depend partially on how many initiatives you need to weigh, as well as the data you use in your calculations. Don't be afraid to start small with a simple scoring method, however, if access to data is a bottleneck.

A Prioritization Model to Consider

The simple prioritization model that I've used in many situations is based on considering a few key factors:

- a. Benefit to business
- b. Benefit to customer
- c. Amount (percent) of audience it affects (on a scale of 1–10)
- d. Cost to implement
- e. Cost to measure

Then, a simple formula will give you a prioritization score:

$$a + b + c - d - e$$

Although this has been implemented in several different ways and with varying levels of sophistication, I recommend starting simply and then tailoring the approach more to your needs (e.g., introducing weights to different elements). A spreadsheet that includes a list of efforts you'd like to prioritize can quickly become a ranked list of items if you also use a simple ranking scale (e.g., 1–10).

I included a version of this in my previous book, *Meaningful Measurement of the Customer Experience* (2021), and you can see more about it there, including an illustration of how to do this in spreadsheet form.

A House of the Customer Prioritization Model

I've taken this concept further and built a prioritization model that utilizes the five pillars, roof, and foundation to rank your initiatives.

Although this is more robust than the simpler model I created previously, it ensures a holistic view of the items you want to prioritize. To help, I've also included a simplified version of this prioritization model in the appendix. You can use it as is or modify it to your needs. Whatever approach you use for a prioritization model, I've found that consistently using the same model creates more value over time than frequently changing your approach. You may want to make slight modifications to get the most relevant results, but finding an overall approach and sticking with it will build value over time as you can start to see relative results.

Now that we've talked about how to find where to start, let's talk about how to get started with your prioritized efforts.

Starting with a Pilot Project

There is no better way to learn than to get started with a project or initiative. The risk, however, is creating such a lengthy, resource-intensive undertaking that by the time you know whether it works, you've already sunk considerable costs into it.

Although I truly believe you learn more by failing than succeeding, leaders and stakeholders should be conservative with how company resources are spent. Therefore, creating the smallest possible project—a pilot project or even a minimum viable product—will often help get initiatives like advancing personalization off the ground.

Make sure you pick a pilot project that not only is low effort but also moves toward providing metrics and feedback that speak to bigger organizational KPIs. For instance, if increasing revenue per session is important, create a small pilot project that tests some assumptions around personalization and shopping cart size.

Let's explore pilot projects a bit more now.

Initiatives that require large changes to people, processes, and technology can be difficult to do well, but starting small can be a good path forward for many reasons.

We often talk about doing pilot projects to gain quicker findings and have better opportunities for long-term success. Despite this, there isn't nearly as much written about how to approach those pilot projects.

I will explore three key things to keep in mind as you plan and execute a pilot project for your next large initiative.

Limited but Meaningful

Let's start with a deceptively simple concept. We need to limit the scope of a pilot project to accomplish it in a relatively short amount of time. However, it must also be of high-enough priority that its results are significant to key stakeholders. Wrapped up in that is the inherent idea that the results of the pilot must be measurable and align with KPIs that are meaningful to the executives who sponsored it. Let's unpack this a little bit more.

Ensure that you create a solid hypothesis and visualize the results a successful pilot should garner. This will help you not only get the buy-in you need but serve as your guide as you build your minimum requirements to achieve this goal. Ultimately, these guidelines will allow you to compare your results to your original hypothesis and see where you went right and where the project needs improvement.

Do this well, or you may not get an opportunity to extend your pilot.

Remember Your Pilot Team

Much of the talk around pilot projects revolves around scope, budget, results, and of course, the all-important leadership buy-in. Although all of those are critical, don't forget another extremely important aspect: the teams that will be creating, implementing, and initially using the pilot initiative.

Organizational change is never simple, but getting the people part of the equation right must not be overlooked. If you are asking a team to build a solution, make sure you get the team that will use that solution involved in the planning, requirement-gathering, and implementation.

Creating a pilot initiative means that it isn't simply a change that will happen once it's launched, but instead the process of creating a pilot is part of the change. Anyone involved in a pilot project is part of an advance team that is there to build it from the ground up. It is *their* pilot just as much as it is yours. This is absolutely the way it should be too. Successful pilot leaders have egos checked at the door and recognize the project is a team effort through and through.

Plan for Success—and the Next Steps

Going from initial planning to pitching your idea internally to designing, building, and launching your pilot project is a lot of work. If it is successful, however, your work is just beginning!

When you achieve success, make sure you have a follow-up plan of what to do next. Momentum is important, and having a prioritized fast-follow list will help save time and effort, reducing the feeling that you have to start from scratch.

Don't forget to have a retrospective to learn from what worked well and what didn't, but be organized in how you embrace success so you can quickly move to the next phase.

Bringing a pilot project to successful completion is no small feat. It takes buy-in from the top as well as from those that will live with the output. It takes focus on the scope needed to achieve the necessary results, and when it succeeds, it requires solid next steps. I wish you much success as you proceed with your next pilot!

Sustaining and Improving with a Center of Experience

So far in this chapter, we've looked at several ways to implement and sustain a House of the Customer of your own. We talked about process-driven approaches and how to measure your progress by utilizing a maturity model.

To ensure there are formal structures around how these things are implemented, it becomes necessary to put something in place to support, enforce, and advocate for continued improvements and resources. In my experience, the best method is to utilize the Center of Experience model to bring together a cross-disciplinary team sanctioned by executive leadership to accomplish specific goals directly tied to organizational KPIs (Figure 3.4.1).

Figure 3.4.1, The Center of Experience Model

For a much more in-depth look at this, I recommend you read my book *The Center of Experience: A Blueprint for Creating the Experience-led Enterprise* (2019) because it goes through how to think about each element piece by piece. It also features a framework for an experience maturity scale that can measure both customer and employee experience.

Adding Business Experience to the Center of Experience

There is a third element we can and should introduce to our Center of Experience, and that is *business experience*. It's similar to customer and employee experience yet distinct. When I interviewed Leon Gilbert, senior vice president and general manager at Unisys Digital Workspace Solutions, for *The Agile Brand* podcast, he had this to say:

Business experience, in very simple terms, is the reason why an organization exists. For example, the desired business experience for a pharmaceutical might be something like, "Let's safely create and sell new drugs to make a profit whilst beating all the major competition to the market." When a pharma achieves this, the company has that great business experience, and obviously the shareholders do as well. But to really achieve this desired experience, the company has to implement several key business initiatives. And as an example . . . to set up and create new drugs, they may have to go and acquire a small startup. They may have to collaborate with educational facilities such as a university on R&D, or they may have to partner with a large hospital to perform clinical trials.

So, whether it's in the pharmaceutical industry or whether it's in any other type of industry—you know, banking, manufacturing, retail, hospitality, et cetera—every organization has a desire for that true business experience and to provide unique kinds of business initiatives. But if you then start to link the business experience to the employee experience, that is when you will get true customer experience.[178]

Although I believe that the Center of Experience model can work for many types and sizes of organizations, I also acknowledge that it may not be the right fit or timing for *every* organization. Additionally, a Center of Experience could be a North Star of its own that you're working toward, but it needs some incremental steps along the way. Because of all of this, I will provide several alternatives below.

Alternatives to a Center of Experience

For organizations that don't have the resources to invest in a Center of Excellence approach or need to prove the model before making such an investment, here are a few ways to think about building toward a Center of Experience.

Project Teams

The first is the smallest of the team- or people-based groups. For organizations on the low end of the maturity scale and therefore primarily engaging in proofs of concept or pilot projects, it may make sense to start with project teams that consist of a few individuals from different disciplines that focus on a goal related to creating more sophisticated personalized customer experiences.

Although project teams are nimble and relatively easy to put together, they lack a formal long-term structure and accountability beyond an initial set of deliverables. For this reason, they are helpful to a point but need to be a stepping stone for something more sustainable.

Working Groups

To take things one step further, an informal working group that convenes as needed and is aligned around a few projects or initiatives could be a good fit.

Organizations that are a little further along on the House of the Customer maturity scale should at least have a working group formed to have conversations about how individual initiatives are lining up with larger strategic objectives.

This working group could just as easily disband when you are done with a particular project, or it could evolve into a steering committee (which we'll discuss next) or even a Center of Excellence.

Working groups can be incredibly effective, but because of their informality and lack of structure, it can be difficult to sustain them. Leadership support is needed for working groups but they often lack a true governance structure or formalized support among leaders. For this reason, they are a great way to get started, but once successful, there should be plans to create a more formal structure for them. This leads us to the next concept.

Steering Committees

Steering committees are the most formal of the alternatives to a Center of Excellence or Center of Experience. They share some characteristics of a Center of Excellence:

- Formalized structure
- Broad executive stakeholder support from multiple departments and teams
- Governance processes
- Accountability for actions and outcomes that are tied to organizational KPIs

This helps solve some of the internal cross-team collaboration challenges discussed earlier. Doing personalized CX well means working across practice areas and departments, often at a national or global level. Therefore, creating a team that meets regularly to discuss personalization goals and how they will be implemented as an enterprise can ensure alignment and assist long-term success.

For organizations that want to emphasize the importance of personalization, a personalization Center of Excellence could be created. This would include stakeholders from the various teams that meet on a regular basis with a formalized mission and set of objectives.

For the greatest success, ensure multiple executives support the effort and that a formalized structure provides representation from key teams on the committee. Draw up a charter that guides activities, and make sure there are opportunities to present progress to leadership and the company at large.

Measuring Growth

Finally, it is imperative that you take a bird's-eye view of measuring your organization's growth. This is where the maturity model mentioned in chapter 2.5.2 comes into play. Set a current state and the desired state, and try to see how your organization fits within your competitive set.

This maturity model and measurements can be your gauge of growth and a reminder that continuous improvement is needed to stay competitive. Make sure to check out the more detailed view provided in the appendix of this book and in the downloadable materials online at https://www.houseofthecustomer.com/.

Conclusion

For fans of home improvement, the road ahead looks full of interesting challenges and learning opportunities. For those who are anxious about continual change, the gradual, iterative methods described can be a great way to ensure that the needed change is handled in a manageable way.

Either way, we know one thing: change is the only certainty, whether from external factors or internal ones. How we work together and pull our people, processes, and platforms together can make the difference between success and failure.

Conclusion

When you are finished changing, you are finished.
—Benjamin Franklin

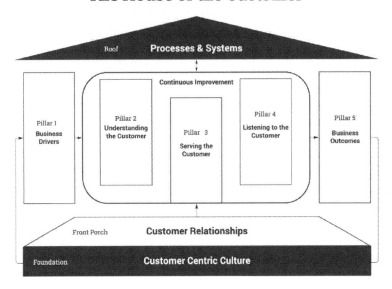

Figure 4.1, The House of the Customer

We are at the end of this book, but you are at the beginning of your and your organization's next steps to build a customer-centric organization driven by engaged employees. We've explored a lot, including the seven components of a House of the Customer that comprise everything from strategic objectives; methods used to understand, listen to, and serve customers; business outcomes; business culture; and the customer relationships we need to achieve sustainable growth.

This is a book about transforming your organization and the way you reach your customers. It's also about the way you work internally with your team members and leadership as well as the way you do that work. All of this requires the right mindset for today and tomorrow.

When I interviewed Alex Atzberger, CEO of Optimizely, I asked him to describe the mindset of a brand that truly embraces the approaches needed for this type of transformation. Here's what he said:

> *It starts with having a mindset of learning and evolution and that you need to drive digital maturity in terms of your own organization's current state. Do you have a mindset of building not for perfection but for speed and ultimately recognizing that it's not the size of your company that matters?*
>
> *Agility and the speed at which you can move matters in today's market, so there's a lot of similarities between the companies and brands that get it. You see it in terms of the people they hire, and you see it in terms of the initiatives that they take on to improve.*[179]

Here are just a few things to remember before we wrap up here.

Build from Scratch, Remodel, or Clean House?

Start the next part of your journey realistically. Look at your organizational maturity and chart a course that recognizes the good and bad of where you are and sets a course toward where you want to be.

You may need to start from scratch, you may need to remodel the house you're currently in, or you may just need to stay vigilant and keep the good thing you have up to date. Wherever you sit, there is work to be done, and it takes an engaged team to do it.

Let Your North Star Guide You

Finally, let's go back to one of the first concepts we explored together. I highlighted several North Star goals to strive for as you build your House of the Customer. Although many of your desired business outcomes, goals, and KPIs will be unique to your organization, these North Star goals will guide you toward becoming the type of customer-centric company that achieves sustainable success and pulls away from the competition.

It can be easy to get distracted by day-to-day challenges, internal constraints, and other issues, but don't forget that customer expectations continue to grow, and your competition continues to evolve. Building your House of the Customer on a solid foundation with the vision and resources to improve it over time will bring you the long-term success you're after.

Thanks again for exploring this with me. I wish you the best as you build your own House of the Customer. Please share your progress as you build!

Appendix

Although I covered these tools and resources earlier in the book, this appendix will go into more specific detail about each of the four tools mentioned. There have been a few other tools referred to that are available in some of my other books as well.

Printed versions of these tools are available in the pages that follow, but the digital versions of these materials are available at https://www.houseofthecustomer.com/

I hope you find these tools useful and valuable, and feel free to modify them to fit your needs. I'd also love to hear from you if you have feedback or success stories!

Not Included in This Book

There are a few resources I shared in earlier books that I want to highlight but won't be sharing in more depth in this book. These include the Organizational Culture Framework and the Simple Prioritization Model.

Organizational Culture Framework

For more information about this framework, I recommend you read my book *The Center of Experience* (2020), where I detail it in depth and provide a sample assessment to utilize it. I also provide workshops and additional training on this framework. It is based on existing research and a framework called the Competing Values Framework with some modifications.

Simple Prioritization Model

Also from *The Center of Experience* comes a simplified yet effective prioritization model in chapter 3.5. The more robust framework is tied to the House of the Customer model and offers more flexibility and nuance. However, for many prioritization exercises, this simple model is more than adequate for the job. I've used it many times in many settings, and it's never disappointed!

Appendix 1: Maturity Model

The first reference item I've included in the appendix is the House of the Customer Maturity Model that I referenced when talking about our fifth pillar, Business Outcomes. It is important to understand not only how your organization performs at a particular point in time, but also how it progresses toward greater maturity. This is where maturity models come into play, and I've found them incredibly helpful in my work with organizations of all sizes and levels of maturity.

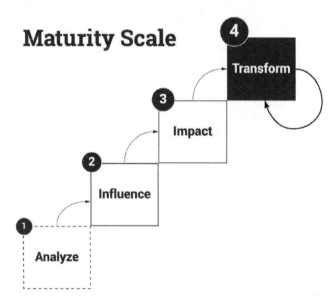

Figure A1.1, The House of the Customer Maturity Scale

The scale that I use in this book has four stages and is based on the elements of our House of the Customer. For a definition of each of the four stages of maturity as well as how your organization stacks up, go to chapter 2.5.2 to see the results of applying this maturity scale across nineteen different research studies over the last three years.

Criteria, Questions, and Scoring

To measure your own organization, I've provided the questions and scoring framework for the House of the Customer maturity model that you can download as a spreadsheet from the online materials available at https://www.houseofthecustomer.com/.

How to Use the Maturity Assessment

The best way to use the maturity assessment is to survey key individuals that know the areas covered. It is best served in a way where respondents can choose a number on a 1–5 rating scale for each element. These are then calculated and averaged to determine a score.

The assessment isn't meant to be an exact measure of the elements of the House of the Customer, so it is best used as a measure relative to both the moment the survey is given, as well as when the survey is given over time.

I recommend that you set a realistic goal and use the maturity assessment to gauge how your teams are progressing toward that goal. In that scenario, sending this survey every six months or once annually would give a good indication of your trajectory toward your goals.

Approach and Methodology

To help you better understand where other organizations fit in the maturity scale, I have compiled research and maturity studies from nineteen other sources over the last three years to provide a more comprehensive view. The scores for overall experience maturity are shown below:

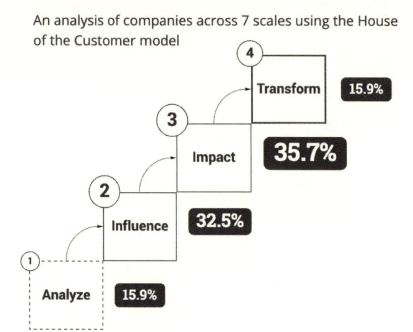

Figure A1.3, Overall Personalized Experience Maturity

The surveys and research that follow these paragraphs were utilized where applicable to compile the average scores for each pie chart in chapter 2.5.2. I prioritized studies that were done in the last two years; only a few are older than that to address a lack of more-recent data. I also endeavored to find research based on studies with an adequate number of responses and sufficient methodological rigor. I don't have firsthand knowledge of the research methods other than what is cited in the reports but have done my best to ensure the integrity of the numbers I present in this book.

Averages of scores found in these reports were made under each of the respective areas, with no fewer than three reports used for each set of criteria, and sometimes many more than that. For overall maturity, I used an average of scores specifically referenced as "overall maturity" from several, as well as the average of all scores of the other criteria. In many reports, overall maturity was treated as a separate and distinct metric. For the purposes of this book and this maturity model, I felt that overall maturity should reflect an average of all key areas, not simply a single subjectively acquired metric on overall progress toward greater maturity.

Here is a list of the references used to compile the industry average scores that were shown in chapter 2.5.2:

1. Accenture. "The Future of Work: Productive Anywhere." April 2021.
2. Ascend2 and SharpSpring. "The State of Marketing and Sales Alignment 2022: How companies are driving growth with a seamless customer experience." 2022.
3. Andrus, Garth R., Gerald C. Kane, Anh Nguyen Phillips, and Jonathan R. Copulsky. "The Technology Fallacy: How People Are The Real Key to Digital Transformation." MIT Press. April 16, 2019.
4. Clevertouch and the University of Southampton. "The State of Martech 2022 Summary Report." 2022.
5. Deloitte Digital. "On the Pulse of Digitalization: Deloitte Digital Maturity Index." 2022.
6. Forrester Research Commissioned by Amperity. "Evolve Your Data Practices to Stay Ahead of the Competition." June 2022.
7. Hotjar. "Hotjar 2020 State of CX Report." 2020.
8. London Research with Netcel, Optimizely, and Siteimprove. "From Digital Transformation to Digital Evolution: Survival of the Quickest." 2022.
9. Patel, Shilpa, Dominic Field, and Henry Leon for Boston Consulting Group. "Responsible Marketing with First-Party Data."
10. Phelps, Nicholas and Forrester's Customer Insights Professionals Research Group for Forrester Research and Tealium. "Customer Data Maturity Powers the Modern Enterprise: Evaluate Your Customer Data Strategy to Plot a Course for the Future of Your Business." 2019.
11. Qualtrics CX Institute State of CX Maturity 2021

12. Rogers, Kristi, Javier Pérez-Moiño, Henry Leon, and Alberto Poncela for Boston Consulting Group. "The Fast Track to Digital Marketing Maturity." 2021.
13. Simon Data. "2022 State of Customer Data: The latest trends in data & usage in a privacy-centric world." 2022.
14. Temkin, Bruce and Maggie Mead for Qualtricx XM Institute. "The State of Customer Experience Management, 2019." 2019.
15. Topline Strategy Group. "NPS Benchmark Fall 2020." https://toplinestrategy.com/topline-releases-updated-nps-b2b-benchmarks/topline-nps-benchmark-fall-2020/ November 2020.
16. Treasure Data. "Where Does Your Business Rank on the Customer Data Maturity Model?" 2022. https://blog.treasuredata.com/blog/2022/02/09/customer-data-maturity-model-cdp-use/
17. UserTesting. "2022 CX Industry Report." 2022.
18. Twilio. "State of Customer Engagement Report 2022." 2022.
19. Zendesk. "CX Trends 2022: Improve Your Bottom Line by Putting Customers at the Top." 2022.

Appendix 2: House of the Customer Prioritization Model

Using the elements of the House of the Customer as measurement points, this prioritization model allows you to take a set of new initiatives and evaluate them with these seven elements:

1. Customer-centric culture
2. Business drivers
3. Understanding the customer
4. Serving the customer
5. Listening to the customer
6. Business outcomes
7. Customer relationships

There are two sides to each of the seven elements, one that is positive and one that is negative. Each of these is also weighted by its benefit to the business. For instance, consistency of customer experience may be a high-priority item, while the cost to measure outcomes may be a lower priority. Then, each initiative is weighted by its potential benefit to customers. Finally, a prioritization score is provided for each item in your list.

A working version of the spreadsheet used to calculate these values is available with the other downloadable materials from this book at https://www.houseofthecustomer.com/.

How to Use the Prioritization Model

1. *Adjust the House of the Customer criteria.* First, assign the "Benefit to Business" criteria according to each element in row 3 of the spreadsheet. This will give you a relative weight for each.

2. *Add Your Potential Initiatives.* Add your potential initiatives and priorities in column C. Choose a value in column C that most accurately reflects the value of each campaign and priority for the customer.
3. *Identify the "Prioritization Score" in column A.* Determining this value will help you set the priorities of initiatives and projects listed in column C.

I hope that you find this prioritization model useful. I have found that, although it takes a bit of setting up, it can be incredibly beneficial when you have a complex list of tasks and initiatives and need an objective view of where to invest time and resources for the greatest impact.

References

1. Kaszubowska, Joanna. "Masterpiece Story: Fallingwater by Frank Lloyd Wright." Daily Art Magazine. August 2, 2022. https://www.dailyartmagazine.com/fallingwater-frank-lloyd-wright/ Retrieved 09-24-2022.
2. Fawcett, Kirstin. "12 Facts About Frank Lloyd Wright's Fallingwater." Mental Floss. January 25, 2017. Retrieved 09-24-2022. https://www.mentalfloss.com/article/90823/12-facts-about-frank-lloyd-wrights-fallingwater
3. Jim Morris, "History of Fallingwater by Architect Frank Lloyd Wright," Archute, September 22, 2021, accessed September 24, 2022. https://www.archute.com/history-fallingwater-frank-lloyd-wright/.
4. Twombly, Robert (1979). Frank Lloyd Wright His Life and Architecture. Canada: A Wiley-Interscience. pp. 276–278.
5. Nielsen. "Annual Marketing Report: Era of Alignment: Future-focused strategies for brand building and customer acquisition" April 2022.
6. Internet Advertising Bureau (IAB). "Study Finds Internet Economy Grew Seven Times Faster Than Total U.S. Economy, Created Over 7 Million Jobs in the Last Four Years." IAB.com. October 18, 2021. https://www.iab.com/news/study-finds-internet-economy-grew-seven-times-faster/ Retrieved 09-24-2022.
7. Joint Economic Committee Democrats. "JEC Report Shows New Business Applications Reached Highest Level on Record." IJEC website. May 5, 2022. https://www.jec.senate.gov/public/index.cfm/democrats/2022/5/jec-report-shows-new-business-applications-reached-highest-level-on-record#:~:text=Americans%20submitted%205.4%20million%20applications,five%20years%20before%20the%20pandemic. Twilio. "State of Customer Engagement Report 2022." 2022.
8. Bureau of Labor and Statistics. "Monthly Business Applications" Retrieved 08-23-2022 https://www.census.gov/econ/bfs/index.html
9. Fontanella, Clint. "9 Customer Experience Trends and Stats That'll Define the Next Year." Hubspot blog. April 18, 2022. https://blog.hubspot.com/service/customer-experience-trends
10. "Cultivating Worker Well-Being to Drive Business Value," Indeed, accessed October 17, 2022. https://www.indeed.com/lead/workforce-well-being-report
11. "Littlest Skyscraper". Wichita Falls Times Record News. Wichita Falls, Texas: E. W. Scripps Company. December 30, 2000. p. 9. ISSN 0895-6138. Retrieved October 9, 2010.
12. Jerome Pohlen (2006). Oddball Texas: A Guide To Some Really Strange Places. Chicago, Illinois: Chicago Review Press. p. 67. ISBN 978-1-55652-583-4.
13. Twilio. State of Customer Engagement Report 2022.
14. Zendesk. CX Trends 2022: Improve Your Bottom Line by Putting Customers at the Top."

Released in 2022.
15. The Agile Brand with Greg Kihlström podcast featuring Paulette Chafe of Zendesk. https://www.gregkihlstrom.com/theagilebrandpodcast/strengthening-business-customer-first April 15, 2022.
16. Prakel, David (10 December 2009). The Visual Dictionary of Photography. AVA Publishing. p. 91. ISBN 978-2-940411-04-7. Retrieved 24 July 2013.
17. Mary Ellen Cagnassola and Lauren Giella, "Fact Check: Did Blockbuster Turn Down Chance to Buy Netflix For $50 Million," Newsweek, accessed October 17, 2022. https://www.newsweek.com/fact-check-did-blockbuster-turn-down-chance-buy-netflix-50-million-1575557?
18. Jim Zarroli, "IBM Turns 100: The Company That Reinvented Itself," NPR Business, Accessed October 17, 2022. https://www.npr.org/2011/06/16/137203529/ibm-turns-100-the-company-that-reinvented-itself
19. Tegan Jones, "The Surprisingly Long History of Nintendo," Gizmodo, accessed October 17, 2022. http://gizmodo.com/the-surprisingly-long-history-of-nintendo-1354286257
20. "Industry Profiles: Video Game Rentals," Encyclopedia.com, accessed October 17, 2022.
21. Salesforce. "Marketing Intelligence Report, Third Edition." April 2022.
22. "Spending on Customer Experience Technologies Will Reach $641 Billion in 2022, According to New IDC Spending Guide," Business Wire, accessed October 17, 2022. https://www.businesswire.com/news/home/20190806005070/en/Spending-on-Customer-Experience-Technologies-Will-Reach-641-Billion-in-2022-According-to-New-IDC-Spending-Guide.
23. "Customer Experience Management Market Size, Share & Trends Analysis Report By Analytical Tools, By Touch Point Type, By Deployment, By End-use, By Region, And Segment Forecasts, 2022 – 2030," Grand View Research, accessed October 17, 2022. https://www.grandviewresearch.com/industry-analysis/customer-experience-management-market.
24. Andrew Fazekas, "North Star Closer to Earth Than Thought," National Geographic, accessed October 17, 2022. https://www.nationalgeographic.com/adventure/article/121204-north-star-distance-closer-solar-system-space-science
25. Chris Pemberton, "Key Findings From the Gartner Customer Service Survey," Gartner, accessed October 17, 2022. https://www.gartner.com/en/marketing/insights/articles/key-findings-from-the-gartner-customer-experience-survey
26. "87 percent of companies state they provide excellent CX, only 11 percent of customers agree," Business Wire, accessed October 17, 2022. https://www.businesswire.com/news/home/20220121005224/en/87-percent-of-companies-state-they-provide-excellent-CX-only-11-percent-of-customers-agree
27. "What Are Customer Expectations, and How Have They Changed?" Salesforce, accessed October 17, 2022. http://www.salesforce.com/research/customer-expectations/
28. "What is GDPR, the EU's new data protection law?" GDPR, EU, accessed October 17, 2022. https://gdpr.eu/what-is-gdpr/
29. "2019 is the Year of . . . CCPA? [Infographic]," The National Law Review, accessed October 17, 2022. https://www.natlawreview.com/article/2019-year-ccpa-infographic
30. "Wealth Management Digitalization changes client advisory more than ever before," Deloitte, accessed October 17, 2022: https://www2.deloitte.com/content/dam/Deloitte/de/Documents/WM%20Digitalisierung.pdf

31. "The Value of Experience: How the C-suite values customer experience in the digital age," The Economist Intelligence Unit, accessed October 17, 2022
32. Forrester Research. "The Total Economic Impact™ Methodology: A foundation for Sound Technology Investments." August 2008.
33. Twilio. State of Customer Engagement Report. 2022.
34. Anh Thi, Van Nguyen, Robert McClelland, Nguyen Hoang Thuan, "Exploring customer experience during channel switching in omnichannel retailing context: A qualitative assessment," Journal of Retailing and Consumer Services, accessed October 17, 2022. https://www.sciencedirect.com/science/article/abs/pii/S0969698921003696
35. Forrester. "The Data Deprecation Challenge and the Promise of Zero-Party Data." 2022.
36. Sailthru, Liveclicker, and Coresight Research. "Retail Personalization in 2022: Balancing Trust, Data Collection, and Privacy." April 2022.
37. Brian Gregg, Hussein Kalaoui, Joel Maynes, and Gustavo Schuler, "Marketing's Holy Grail: Digital Marketing at Scale," McKinsey Digital, accessed October 18, 2022. https://www.mckinsey.com/business-functions/mckinsey-digital/our-insights/marketings-holy-grail-digital-personalization-at-scale
38. Forrester. "The Data Deprecation Challenge and the Promise of Zero-Party Data." 2022.
39. IAB. Internet Advertising Revenue Report Full Year 2021. April 2022.
40. Kif Leswing, "Facebook Says Apple iOS privacy change will result in $10 billion revenue hit this year," CNBC, accessed October 18, 2022. https://www.cnbc.com/2022/02/02/facebook-says-apple-ios-privacy-change-will-cost-10-billion-this-year.html
41. Insider Intelligence and Experian. "Ad Measurement 2022: The Start of a New Era Measuring Video." April 2022.
42. Interactive Advertising Bureau (IAB). "State of Data Report." February 8, 2022.
43. Mediaocean. "H1 2022 Market Report." 2022.
44. Emodo Institute. "Voice of the Marketer Series: Marketers' Perspectives on the Loss of Device Identifies." July 2022.
45. Nielsen. "Annual Marketing Report: Era of Alignment: Future-focused strategies for brand building and customer acquisition" April 2022.
46. Nielsen. "Annual Marketing Report: Era of Alignment: Future-focused strategies for brand building and customer acquisition" April 2022.
47. The Agile Brand with Greg Kihlström podcast featuring Anthony Coppedge, IBM. December 10, 2021. https://www.gregkihlstrom.com/theagilebrandpodcast?offset=1639464720995
48. Sam Daley, "What Is Company Culture?" BuiltIn, accessed October 18, 2022, https://builtin.com/company-culture
49. "Customer Centricity," Gartner, accessed June 20, 2022. https://www.gartner.com/en/marketing/glossary/customer-centricity
50. APA 2018 Work and Well-Being Survey
51. "State Job Openings and Labor Turnover Summary," U.S. Bureau of Labor Statistics, accessed October 18, 2022. https://www.bls.gov/news.release/jltst.nr0.htm
52. "CX stats and trends," Hotjar, accessed October 18, 2022. https://www.hotjar.com/customer-experience/trends-and-stats/
53. The Agile Brand with Greg Kihlström podcast featuring Paulette Chafe of Zendesk. https://www.gregkihlstrom.com/theagilebrandpodcast/strengthening-business-customer-first April

15, 2022.
54. The Agile Brand with Greg Kihlström podcast with guest John Nash, Redpoint Global. https://www.theagilebrand.show 2022
55. Lacek Group and Sitecore. "The Changing Look of Loyalty." April 2022.
56. "Forbes Insight Experience Equation Final Report," Salesforce, accessed October 18, 2022. https://www.salesforce.com/content/dam/web/en_us/www/documents/reports/forbes-insight%20experienceequation%20final-report.pdf Greg Kihlström, interview with Paulette Chafe of Zendesk, The Agile Brand with Greg Kihlström, podcast audio, April 15, 2022, https://www.gregkihlstrom.com/theagilebrandpodcast/strengthening-business-customer-first.
57. Greg Kihlström, interview with Sami Nuwar, Director, Customer Experience Advisory at Medallia, The Agile Brand with Greg Kihlström, podcast audio, March 15, 2022, https://www.gregkihlstrom.com/theagilebrandpodcast/cx-skeptics
58. Greg Kihlström, interview with Leon Gilbert, Unisys, The Agile Brand with Greg Kihlström, podcast audio, February 15, 2022, https://www.gregkihlstrom.com/theagilebrandpodcast/business-experience-employee-experience.
59. Greg Kihlström, interview with Steve Petruk, CGS, The Agile Brand with Greg Kihlström featuring Steve Petruk, podcast audio, March 4, 2022, https://www.gregkihlstrom.com/theagilebrandpodcast/people-process-technology-2.
60. Kate Taylor, "Chick-fil-A continues to dominate customer satisfaction rankings as the fast-food chain takes over America," Business Insider, accessed October 18, 2022. https://www.businessinsider.com/chick-fil-a-dominates-customer-satisfaction-rankings-2020-6.
61. "Customer satisfaction benchmarks and strategic insights for fast food restaurants," ACSI, accessed October 18, 2022. https://www.theacsi.org/industries/restaurant/fast-food/.
62. Accenture. "The Future of Work: Productive Anywhere." May 2021.
63. Fowell, Tiffany. "What is hybrid work and why do employees want it?" May 11, 2022. Envoy Blog. https://envoy.com/blog/what-is-a-hybrid-work-model/
64. Day, George S. "Innovation Prowess: Leadership Strategies for Accelerating Growth." Wharton School Press. April 16, 2013.
65. London Research, Netcel, Optimizely, Siteimprove. "From Digital Transformation to Digital Evolution: Survival of the Quickest." June 2022.
66. Greg Kihlström, interview with Alex Atzenberger, CEO of Optimizely, The Agile Brand with Greg Kihlström, podcast audio, December 7, 2021, https://www.gregkihlstrom.com/theagilebrandpodcast/adapting-customer-expectations-alex-atzberger.
67. "'Move Fast and Break Things': Pros and Cons of the Concept," MasterClass, accessed October 19, 2022. https://www.masterclass.com/articles/move-fast-and-break-things
68. Greg Kihlström, interview with Judy Bloch, Medallia, The Agile Brand with Greg Kihlström, podcast audio, September 12, 2022, https://www.gregkihlstrom.com/the-agile-brand-blog/2022/9/12/driving-change-to-have-more-successful-cx-programs-with-judy-bloch-medallia
69. London Research, Netcel, Optimizely, Siteimprove. "From Digital Transformation to Digital Evolution: Survival of the Quickest." June 2022.
70. "Despite Disengagement at Work, 65% of Employees Plan to Stay in Their Current Jobs According to New Achievers Study," Cision PR Newswire, accessed October 19, 2022. https://www.prnewswire.com/news-releases/despite-disengagement-at-work-65-of-employees-planto-stay-in-their-current-jobs-according-to-new-achievers-study-300810391.html

71. "Managing Employee Surveys," SHRM, accessed October 19, 2022. https://www.shrm.org/resourcesandtools/tools-and-samples/toolkits/pages/managingemployeesurveys.aspx
72. "10 Timely Statistics About the Connections Between Employee Engagement and Wellness," Forbes, accessed October 19, 2022. https://www.forbes.com/sites/nazbeheshti/2019/01/16/10-timely-statistics-about-the-connectionbetween-employee-engagement-and-wellness/?
73. Greg Kihlström , interview with Tim Brackney, President and COO of RGP, The Agile Brand with Greg Kihlström, podcast audio, August 9, 2022, https://www.gregkihlstrom.com/theagilebrandpodcast/remote-work-culture
74. Jeff Degraff, Robert E. Quinn, Anjan V. Thakor, Kim S. Cameron, Competing Values Leadership: Creating Value in Organizations (Elgar Publishing, Inc., 2007).
75. Susan Harrington, Tor Guimaraes, "Corporate Culture, Absorptive Capcity, and IT Success," October 2004.
76. Harvey, M., Palmer, J., & Speier, C. (1998). Implementing intra-organizational learning: A phased-model approach supported by intranet technology. European Management Journal, 16(3), June, 341-354.
77. Greg Kihlström, interview with Jon Ebert of John Deere, The Agile Brand with Greg Kihlström, podcast audio, March 18, 2022, https://www.gregkihlstrom.com/theagilebrandpodcast/innovation-storytelling.
78. Kane, Gerald C., Anh Nguyeyn Philips, Jonathan R. Copulsky, and Garth R. Andrus. "The Technology Fallacy: How People are the Real Key to Digital Transformation." MIT Press. April 2019.
79. Zendesk. "CX Trends 2022: Improve Your Bottom Line by Putting Customers at the Top." 2022.
80. Zendesk. "CX Trends 2022: Improve Your Bottom Line by Putting Customers at the Top." 2022.
81. Kaminski, Andre. "Measuring Business Value in DevOps and Agile Projects." LinkedIn. April 14, 2019. https://www.linkedin.com/pulse/measuring-business-value-devops-agile-projects-andre-kaminski/ Sourced on June 20, 2022.
82. Greg Kihlström, interview with Sara Taheri, Prudential Financial, Inc., The Agile Brand with Greg Kihlström, podcast audio, April 19, 0222, https://www.gregkihlstrom.com/theagilebrandpodcast/people-process-technology-sara-taheri
83. Twilio. "State of Customer Engagement Report 2022." 2022.
84. Nielsen. "Annual Marketing Report: Era of Alignment: Future-focused strategies for brand building and customer acquisition" April 2022.
85. CleverTouch and University of Southampton Business School. "The State of Martech 2022." April 2022.
86. Nielsen. "Annual Marketing Report: Era of Alignment: Future-focused strategies for brand building and customer acquisition" April 2022.
87. The Lacek Group and Sitecore. "The Changing Look of Loyalty." April 2022.
88. Medallia Institute. "Uncovering the Secrets Behind a Successful Customer Experience Program: A study of more than 580 customer experience programs identifies what separates CX leaders from laggards." May 2022.
89. Bree Fowler, "Data breaches break record in 2021," CNET, accessed September 24, 2022. https://www.cnet.com/news/privacy/record-number-of-data-breaches-reported-in-2021-new-report-says/

90. Sailthru, Liveclicker, and Coresight Research. "Retail Personalization in 2022: Balancing Trust, Data Collection and Privacy." April 2022.
91. Forrester and Zeta Global. Forrester Opportunity Snapshot: A Custom Study Commissioned by Zeta Global. April 2022.
92. Forrester and Zeta Global. Forrester Opportunity Snapshot: A Custom Study Commissioned by Zeta Global. April 2022.
93. Forrester and Zeta Global. Forrester Opportunity Snapshot: A Custom Study Commissioned by Zeta Global. April 2022.
94. Commerce Next. "The Ascension to Digital Maturity: A Benchmark Report: Retailers Graduate from Setting Table Stakes to Scaling Long-Term Strategies." June 2022.
95. Forrester and Zeta Global. Forrester Opportunity Snapshot: A Custom Study Commissioned by Zeta Global. April 2022.
96. Forrester and Zeta Global. Forrester Opportunity Snapshot: A Custom Study Commissioned by Zeta Global. April 2022.
97. Forrester Consulting and Google. "Forrester Wave Report.". August 2021. Retrieved 09-24-2022.
98. Appsflyer. "Appsflyer Releases its Data Clean Room." Businesswire. June 7, 2022. https://www.businesswire.com/news/home/20220607005300/en/AppsFlyer-Releases-Its-Data-Clean-Room/ Retrieved 09-24-2022.
99. Forrester Consulting, commissioned by Simon Data. "When Data Drags You Down Report". March 2022.
100. Bond, Steward for IDC. "Improving Data Integrity and Trust Through Transparency and Enrichment." June 2022.
101. Twilio. "State of Customer Engagement Report 2022." 2022.
102. Forrester. "The Data Deprecation Challenge and the Promise of Zero-Party Data." 2022.
103. Nielsen. "Annual Marketing Report: Era of Alignment: Future-focused strategies for brand building and customer acquisition" April 2022.
104. Forrester. "The Data Deprecation Challenge and the Promise of Zero-Party Data." 2022.
105. Lacek Group and Sitecore. "The Changing Look of Loyalty." April 2022.
106. Forrester. "The Data Deprecation Challenge and the Promise of Zero-Party Data". 2022.
107. Frontier Communications. "What is the real value of the online world & digital convenience?" May 2022. https://frontier.com/resources/how-much-is-it-worth-study#/is-the
108. Deloitte, "Changing consumer, digital marketing and impact of COVID-19," Deloitte blog, accessed September 24, 2022. https://www2.deloitte.com/si/en/pages/strategy-operations/articles/changing-consumer-digital-marketing-impact-Covid-19.html.
109. Twilio. "State of Customer Engagement Report 2022." 2022.
110. Accenture Interactive, "Making it Personal: Why Brands Must Move from Communication to Conversation for Greater Personalization," Accenture Pulse Survey, 2018.
111. "The power of me: The impact of personalization on marketing performance," Epsilon and Conversant, January 9, 2018.
112. Nidhi Arora, et al., "The Value of Getting Personalization Right—or wrong—is multiplying," McKinsey & Company blog, accessed October 19, 2022. https://www.mckinsey.com/business-functions/marketing-and-sales/our-insights/the-value-of-getting-personalization-right-or-wrong-is-multiplying
113. Salesforce, "Personalization Defined: What is Personalization?" Salesforce blog, accessed June

23, 2022. https://www.salesforce.com/resources/articles/personalization-definition/.
114. "What is the real value of the online world & digital convenience?" Frontier Communications, accessed October 19, 2022. https://frontier.com/resources/how-much-is-it-worth-study#/is-the.
115. Campaign Monitor, "The Power of Email Personalization to Reach Humans (Not Just Inboxes)," Campaign Monitor Blog, accessed September 24, 2022. https://www.campaignmonitor.com/resources/guides/personalized-email/.
116. "2022 Customer Global Customer Engagement Review: Ace your marketing strategy with these proven facts and findings," Braze, 2022.
117. Justina Alexandra Sava, "Share of Customer interactions that are digital, before and during COVID-19 pandemic," Statista, accessed September 24, 2022. https://www.statista.com/statistics/1248804/share-of-customer-interactions-that-are-digital/.
118. Medallia Institute. "Uncovering the Secrets Behind a Successful Customer Experience Program: A study of more than 580 customer experience programs identifies what separates CX leaders from laggards." May 2022.
119. Scott Brinker, "Marketing Technology Landscape Supergraphic (2020)," Chiefmartec, accessed September 24, 2022. https://chiefmartec.com/2020/04/marketing-technology-landscape-2020-martech-5000.
120. CleverTouch. "The State of Martech 2022." April 2022.
121. Forrester. "Customer Data Maturity Powers the Modern Enterprise: Evaluate Your Customer Data Strategy to Plat A Course for the Future of Your Business." January 2019.
122. Salesforce. "Marketing Intelligence Report, Third Edition." April 2022.
123. Braze. "2022 Customer Global Customer Engagement Review: Ace your marketing strategy with these proven facts and findings." 2022.
124. Nord Anglia, "We have two ears and one mouth so that we can listen twice as much as we speak," The British International School Shanghai, Puxi, accessed September 24, 2022. https://www.nordangliaeducation.com/biss-puxi/news/2022/02/22/we-have-two-ears-and-one-mouth-so-that-we-can-listen-twice-as-much-as-we-speak.
125. Salesforce. "Marketing Intelligence Report, Third Edition." April 2022.
126. Insider Intelligence and Experian. "Ad Measurement 2022: The Start of a New Era Measuring Video." April 2022.
127. SharpSpring and Ascend2, "The State of Marketing and Sales Alignment 2022," accessed September 24, 2022. https://ss-usa.s3.amazonaws.com/c/3/media/1627627d9cea9725322594035822947/Sales%20%26%20Marketing%20Alignment%20-%20SharpSpring%20Research%20220426%20FINAL.pdf
128. Nielsen. "Annual Marketing Report: Era of Alignment: Future-focused strategies for brand building and customer acquisition" April 2022.
129. Nielsen. "Annual Marketing Report: Era of Alignment: Future-focused strategies for brand building and customer acquisition" April 2022.
130. SharpSpring and Ascend2, "The State of Marketing and Sales Alignment 2022," accessed September 24, 2022. https://ss-usa.s3.amazonaws.com/c/3/media/1627627d9cea9725322594035822947/Sales%20%26%20Marketing%20Alignment%20-%20SharpSpring%20Research%20220426%20FINAL.pdf
131. Anh Thi, Van Nguyen, RobertMcClelland, Nguyen Hoang Thuan, "Exploring customer experience during channel switching in omnichannel retailing context: A qualitative assessment," Journal of Retailing and Consumer Services , accessed October 17, 2022.

https://www.sciencedirect.com/science/article/abs/pii/S0969698921003696.
132. MMA Global. "State of Attribution Annual Marketer Survey." July 2022.
133. Stephen Hill, "The Best Customer Journeys Are Driven By the Best Customer Service Solutions," accessed May 24, 2022. https://blogs.oracle.com/marketingcloud/post/behold-the-business-value-of-omni-channel-orchestration.
134. Suttida Yang, "How to Successfully Map Out the Buyer Journey," Suttida Yang Blog, accessed September 24, 2022. https://suttida.com/how-to-successfully-map-out-the-buyer-journey/.
135. Dorothea Schmidt, et al., "Wealth Management Digitalization changes client advisory more than ever before: How to serve the unique demands of a challenging new generation of wealthy individuals with smart digitalization of the wealth management value chain," Deloitte, accessed May 22, 2022.
https://www2.deloitte.com/content/dam/Deloitte/de/Documents/WM%20Digitalisierung.pdf.
136. Twilio. "State of Customer Engagement Report 2022." 2022.
137. Zendesk. "CX Trends 2022: Improve Your Bottom Line by Putting Customers at the Top." 2022.
138. Medallia Institute. "Uncovering the Secrets Behind a Successful Customer Experience Program: a Study of more than 580 customer experience programs identifies what separates CX leaders from laggards." 2022.
139. Alexandra Twin, et al., "What Are KPIs?" Investopedia, accessed September 24, 2022. https://www.investopedia.com/terms/k/kpi.asp.
140. Fred Reichheid, "Prescription for Cutting Costs," Bain & Company, accessed June 20, 2022. http://www2.bain.com/Images/BB_Prescription_cutting_costs.pdf.
141. Alexandra Panaitescu, "10 KPIs with a major impact on your Customer Lifetime Value," Omniconvert blog, accessed September 24, 2022. https://www.omniconvert.com/blog/10-kpis-major-impact-customer-lifetime-value/.
142. Forrester. "The Data Deprecation Challenge and the Promise of Zero-Party Data." 2022.
143. Braze. "2022 Customer Global Customer Engagement Review: Ace your marketing strategy with these proven facts and findings." 2022.
144. Sailthru, Liveclicker, and Coresight Research. "Retail Personalization in 2022: Balancing Trust, Data Collection and Privacy." April 2022.
145. Forrester and Zeta Global. Forrester Opportunity Snapshot: A Custom Study Commissioned by Zeta Global. April 2022.
146. Salesforce. "State of the Connected Customer: Insights from nearly 17,000 consumers and business buyers on the new customer engagement landscape, Fifth Edition." 2021.
147. Nick Bunkley, "Joseph Juran, 103, Pioneer in Quality Control, Dies,"The New York Times, March 3, 2008.
148. Twilio. "State of Customer Engagement Report 2022." 2022.
149. Lacek Group and Sitecore. "The Changing Look of Loyalty." April 2022.
150. Greg Kihlström, The Agile Brand with Greg Kihlström, podcast audio, https://www.gregkihlstrom.com/theagileworld.
151. CleverTouch. "The State of Martech 2022." April 2022.
152. Greg Kihlström, interview with Sara Taheri, Prudential Financial, Inc., The Agile Brand with Greg Kihlström, podcast audio, April 19, 0222, https://www.gregkihlstrom.com/theagilebrandpodcast/people-process-technology-sara-taheri.
153. Greg Kihlström, interview with Sami Nuwar, The Agile Brand with Greg Kihlström, podcast

audio, April 4, 2022, https://www.gregkihlstrom.com/the-agile-brand-blog/2022/4/4/winning-over-cx-skeptics-with-sami-nuwar-medallia.

154. Greg Kihlström, interview with Sara Taheri, Prudential Financial, Inc., The Agile Brand with Greg Kihlström, podcast audio, April 19, 0222, https://www.gregkihlstrom.com/theagilebrandpodcast/people-process-technology-sara-taheri.

155. Jaclyn Anglis, "The Terrifying True Story of The Winchester Mystery House and the Troubled Heiress Who Built It," All That's Interesting, accessed September 24, 2022. https://allthatsinteresting.com/winchester-mystery-house.

156. "Sarah Winchester: Woman of Mystery," Winchester Mystery House, LLC, archived from the original on January 28, 2017.

157. "Winchester Mystery House," Frommer's, archived from the original on February 25, 2021.

158. Patrick Forth, "Flipping the Odds of Digital Transformation Success," BCG blog, accessed September 24, 2022. https://www.bcg.com/publications/2020/increasing-odds-of-success-in-digital-transformation.

159. Kirti Sharma, "5 Common Causes of Resistance to Change in Organizations (+ Tips)," Whatfix, accessed September 24, 2022. https://whatfix.com/blog/causes-of-resistance-to-change/.

160. Kubler-Ross E. On Death and Dying. New York: Simon & Schuster, Inc.; 1969.

161. Anastasia Belyh, "Understanding the Kubler-Ross Change Curve," Cleverism, accessed June 12, 2022. https://www.cleverism.com/understanding-kubler-ross-change-curve/.

162. Greg Kihlström, The Agile Brand with Greg Kihlström, podcast audio, https://www.gregkihlstrom.com/theagileworld.

163. Sideways6, "The Top 50 Listening Leaders," Sideways6 blog, accessed September 24, 2022. https://ideas.sideways6.com/article/the-top-50-listening-leaders.

164. Greg Kihlström, interview with John Estafanous, Rallybright , The Agile Brand with Greg Kihlström, podcast audio, May 16, 2022, https://www.gregkihlstrom.com/the-agile-brand-blog/2022/5/16/high-performance-teams-with-john-estafanous-rallybright

165. Optimizely. "Becoming an Adaptive, Outcomes-focused Business: How Brands Can Deliver Excellent Digital Experiences Amid Heightened, Evolving Customer Expectations." 2021.

166. Greg Kihlström , interview with Alex Atzenberger, CEO of Optimizely, The Agile Brand with Greg Kihlström, podcast audio, December 7, 2021, https://www.gregkihlstrom.com/theagilebrandpodcast/adapting-customer-expectations-alex-atzberger.

167. Medallia webinar, featuring Fed Reichheld, Michelle Peluso, and John Abraham. "Leadership, Culture, & Why Loving Your Customers Matters." July 2022.

168. London Research, Netcel, Optimizely, Siteimprove. "From Digital Transformation to Digital Evolution: Survival of the Quickest." June 2022.

169. Mariette Manktelow, "History of Taxonomy," Uppsala University, accessed September 24, 2022. http://www.atbi.eu/summerschool/files/summerschool/Manktelow_Syllabus.pdf.

170. Sandra Knapp, "What's in a name? A history of taxonomy: Linnaeus and the birth of modern taxonomy," Natural History Museum, London, archived from the original on 18 October 2014.

171. Greg Kihlström, interview with Wendy Pravda, Medallia, The Agile World with Greg Kihlström, podcast audio, June 10, 2022, https://www.gregkihlstrom.com/theagilebrandpodcast/customer-experience-governance.

172. Jack Flynn. "25 Amazing Cloud Adoption Statistics [2022]," Zippia, accessed September 24,

2022. https://www.zippia.com/advice/cloud-adoption-statistics/.

173. Matthew Zane, "How Many New Businesses Started in 2021?" Zippia, accessed September 24, 2022. https://www.zippia.com/advice/how-many-new-businesses-started/.

174. Matthew Zane, "How Many New Businesses Started in 2021?" Zippia, accessed September 24, 2022. https://www.zippia.com/advice/how-many-new-businesses-started/.

175. Martech. "MarTech Replacement Survey 2022." July 2022.

176. Greg Kihlström, interview with Jason McClelland, The Agile World with Greg Kihlström, podcast audio, November 26, 2021, https://www.gregkihlstrom.com/theagilebrandpodcast/search-content-discovery-jason-mcclelland.

177. Greg Kihlström, interview with Paulette Chafe of Zendesk, The Agile Brand with Greg Kihlström, podcast audio, April 15, 2022, https://www.gregkihlstrom.com/theagilebrandpodcast/strengthening-business-customer-first.

178. Greg Kihlström, The Agile Brand with Greg Kihlström, podcast audio, https://www.gregkihlstrom.com/theagileworld.

179. Greg Kihlström , interview with Alex Atzenberger, CEO of Optimizely, The Agile Brand with Greg Kihlström, podcast audio, December 7, 2021, https://www.gregkihlstrom.com/theagilebrandpodcast/adapting-customer-expectations-alex-atzberger.

Made in the USA
Columbia, SC
16 January 2023

9e663a7c-a65d-4a1b-b3a4-c8c3c1f3a6f9R01